Introduction

Food Finder

GW00363280

Our choice:

INTRODUCTION

Time for Food guides are designed to help you find interesting and enjoyable places to eat in the world's main tourist destinations. Each guide divides the destination into eight areas. Each area has a map, followed by a selection of the restaurants, cafés, bars, pubs and food markets in that area. The aim is to cover the whole spectrum of food establishments, from gourmet temples to humble cafés, plus good food shops or delicatessens where you can buy picnic ingredients or food to cook yourself.

If you are looking for a particular restaurant, regardless of its location, or a particular type of cuisine, you can turn to the Food Finder, starting on page 4. This lists all the establishments reviewed in this guide by name (in alphabetical order) and then by cuisine type.

PRICES

Unlike some guides, we have not wasted space telling you how bad a restaurant is – bad or poor-value restaurants simply do not make it into the guide. Many other guides ask restaurants to pay for their entries, or expect the restaurant to advertise in return for a listing. We do neither of these things: the restaurants and cafés featured here simply represent a selection of places that the author has sampled and enjoyed.

If there is one consistent criterion for inclusion in the guide, it is good value. Good value does not, of course,

necessarily mean cheap. Food lovers know the difference between a restaurant where the high prices are fully justified by the quality of the ingredients and the excellence of the cooking and presentation of the food, and meretricious establishments where high prices are merely the result of pretentious attitudes.

Some of the restaurants featured here are undeniably expensive if you consume caviar and champagne, but even haute cuisine establishments offer set-price menus (especially at lunchtime) allowing budget diners to enjoy dishes created by top chefs and every bit as good as those on the regular menu. At the same time, some of the eating places listed here might not make it into more conventional food guides, because they are relatively humble cafés or takeaways. Some are deliberately oriented towards tourists, but there is nothing wrong in that: what some guides dismiss as 'tourist traps' may be deservedly popular for providing choice and good value.

FEEDBACK

You may or may not agree with the author's choice – in either case we would like to know about your experiences. Any feedback you give us and any recommendations you make will be followed up, so that you can look forward to seeing your restaurant suggestions in print in the next edition.

Feedback forms have been included at the back of the book and you can e-mail us with comments by writing to: *timeforfood@thomascook.com*. No food guide can keep pace with the changing restaurant scene, as chefs move on, establishments open or close, and menus, opening hours or credit card details change. Let us know what you like or do not like about the restaurants featured here. Tell us if you discover shops, pubs, cafés, bars, restaurants or markets that

you think should go in the guide. Let us know if you discover changes – say to telephone numbers or opening times.

Symbols used in this guide

VISA	Visa accepted
(D)	Diners Club accepted
	MasterCard accepted
	Restaurant
	Bar, café or pub
	Shop, market or picnic site
∅	Telephone
	Transport
2	Numbered red circles relate to the maps at the start of the section

The price indications used in this guide have the following meanings:

€	budget level
€€	typical/average for the destination
€€€	up-market

FOOD FINDER

▲ Sarphati Park

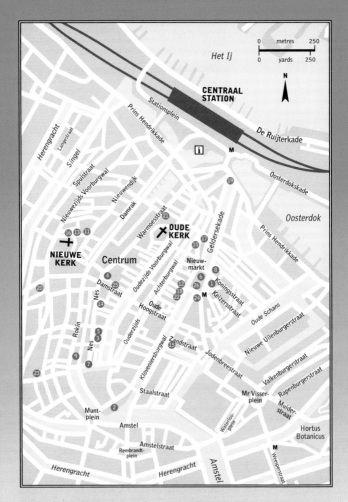

The Old Side and the Dam

The image of the Old Side of Amsterdam is centred on sex and drugs, as here you'll find the Red Light District, but this brash area also has plenty of old buildings, as the name suggests, and several good restaurants, cafés and food shops – not every Amsterdam window contains a woman in her underwear!

THE OLD SIDE AND THE DAM
Restaurants

Café Bern ❶

Nieuwmarkt 9

✆ 622 0034

🚇 Metro to Nieuwmarkt or trams 4, 9, 14, 16, 20, 24 and 25

Open: daily from 1600, food from 1800

Reservations recommended

No credit cards accepted

Swiss

€

Cheese fondue is a Swiss dish which the Dutch – great cheese-lovers – have taken to their hearts, and here is one of the best places to try it, with a busy, casual atmosphere and a well-stocked bar.

Café de Jaren ❷

Nieuwe Doelenstraat 20

✆ 625 5771

🚇 Trams 4, 9, 14, 16, 20, 24 and 25

Open: daily from 1000, food from 1730

Reservations unnecessary

No credit cards accepted

International

€€

This bright and busy café-bar-restaurant is one of the biggest in the city, in a wonderfully-restored old canalside building, with the restaurant serving such straightforward dishes as rib-eye steak. Make sure you get a table overlooking the Amstel.

Café-Restaurant Blincker ❸

St Barberenstraat 7

✆ 627 1938

🚇 Trams 4, 9, 16, 20, 24 and 25

Open: Mon–Sat from 1600

Reservations unnecessary

All credit cards accepted

International

€

You won't find haute cuisine here, but you can be sure of good healthy and tasty food in this trendy place in the **Frascati Theatre** building. Join art and media people dining off

▲ Café de Jaren

▲ In de Waag

soups, pastas, cheese fondue or numerous types of pancake.

Café Roux ④

The Grand, Oudezijds Voorburgwal 197

✆ 555 3111

🚋 Trams 4, 9, 14, 16, 20, 24 and 25

Open: daily for breakfast, lunch and dinner

Reservations recommended

All credit cards accepted

French

€€

The British-based French chef Albert Roux oversees this smart but relaxed brasserie in The Grand hotel, where modern French cuisine is served in art-nouveau surroundings, but at very reasonable prices. One of the city's best food bargains.

Frascati ⑤

Nes 59

✆ 624 1324

🚋 Trams 4, 9, 14, 16, 20, 24 and 25

Open: daily from 1600, food from 1730

Reservations unnecessary

All credit cards accepted

International

€

This plush red bar in the **Frascati Theatre** attracts a bohemian crowd like the nearby **Café-Restaurant Blincker** (see page 9) and serves similar simple but good food, mostly as a background to the drink and chatter.

In de Waag ⑥

Nieuwmarkt 4

✆ 422 7772

Ⓜ Metro to Nieuwmarkt

Open: daily from 1000

Reservations essential in restaurant but unnecessary in café

All credit cards accepted

International

€€

In a fabulous location in the old city gate, a casual café downstairs serves simple fare such as smoked salmon omelette, and a smarter restaurant upstairs offers fancier dishes such as Barbary duck.

La Margarita

Lange Brugsteeg 6

✆ 624 0529

Ⓜ Metro to Centraal Station or trams 1, 2, 4, 5, 9, 13, 14, 16, 17, 20, 24 and 25

Open: Tue–Sun from 1700

Reservations recommended

All credit cards accepted

Mexican

€€

Mexican restaurants are everywhere in Amsterdam and this bright place has proved popular for its huge portions of guacamole, tacos, burritos and other Mexican favourites, while also dishing up good fish dishes and, of course, powerful margaritas.

Nam Kee ⑧

Geldersekade 117

✆ 624 3470

Ⓜ Metro to Nieuwmarkt or trams 4, 9, 16, 20, 24 and 25

Open: daily from 1200

Reservations unnecessary

No credit cards accepted

Chinese

€

One of the best Chinese restaurants in the city, in the heart of Chinatown, this place has an unpretentious décor (some would say scruffy) but an inexpensive and tasty menu that keeps customers returning. Try the steamed duck in a plum sauce.

De Nissen ⑨

Rokin 95

✆ 624 2825

Ⓜ Trams 4, 9, 16, 20, 24 and 25

Open: Mon–Sat 1200–2130

Reservations recommended

All credit cards accepted

Dutch

€€

This venerable Dutch restaurant in an old-fashioned warren-like building has a very relaxed atmosphere. Fish is a speciality of the house, with dishes such as lobster bisque, grilled salmon and other simple but well-done dishes.

Palmers ⑩

Zeedijk 4–8

✆ 427 0551

Ⓜ Trams 1, 2, 4, 5, 9, 13, 14, 17, 20, 24 and 25

Open: daily from 1700

Reservations unnecessary

All credit cards accepted

Dutch

€

The food may not sound out of the ordinary – steaks, fish, *tapas* – but every dish is well-prepared and tasty, and this old bar-restaurant with its low-ceilinged rooms has an atmosphere all of its own in the heart of the old sailors' district.

THE OLD SIDE AND THE DAM
Bars, cafés and pubs

Café Belgique ⑪

Gravenstraat 2

☎ 625 1974

🚊 Trams 1, 2, 5, 13, 14, 17, 20, 24 and 25

Open: daily from 1200

💶

As the name suggests, this is a bar that concentrates on Belgian beers, including Trappist, fruit and wheat beers, and the food includes some Belgian specialities such as a Trappist cheese.

Café 't Loosje ⑫

Nieuwmarkt 32–24

☎ 627 2635

🚊 Metro to Nieuwmarkt or trams 4, 9, 14, 16, 20, 24 and 25

Open: daily from 0930

💶

One of the best places to watch the world go by on the big and bustling Nieuwmarkt, and the world certainly goes by you in Amsterdam. A brown café (*see page 36*)

serving a range of snacks, with a cosy indoors if the weather turns cold, but otherwise plenty of outdoor seating.

De Drie Fleschjes ⑬

Gravenstraat 18

☎ 624 8443

🚊 Trams 1, 2, 4, 5, 9, 13, 16, 20, 24 and 25

Open: Mon–Sat from 1200, Sun from 1500

💶

If you want to try a range of Dutch *jenevers* (gins) – or perhaps just one or two but from a wide choice – then this is the place to come as it has a great selection of flavours, plus beers, wines and liqueurs. Look for the barrels which are padlocked, bought by businesses and individual drinkers for their sole use.

Droesem ⑭

Nes 41

☎ 620 3316

🚊 Trams 4, 9, 14, 16, 20, 24 and 25

Open: daily from 1700

💶

This wine bar close to Dam Square has a good list, though the cheap house wine by the carafe is great value. Simple foods such as soups, cheeses, steaks,

▲ Café 't Loosje

chicken and salmon soak up the alcohol.

Engelbewaarder

Kloveniersburgwal 59

✆ 625 3772

Trams 4, 9, 14, 16, 20, 24 and 25

Open: Mon–Sat from 1200, Sun from 1400

In Amsterdam's wide-ranging list of eating and drinking options, this pleasant place calls itself a beer-café, with a large number of European brews available, basic food and, on Sunday afternoons, live jazz – so get there early.

Henri Prouvin

Gravenstraat 20

✆ 623 9333

Trams 1, 2, 5, 13, 14, 17 and 20

Open: Tue–Sat from 1600

At this slightly more up-market bar in this area renowned for its watering holes, Henri Prouvin concentrates more on wines and champagnes. Many are available just by the glass, and the prices generally suit all pockets.

In't Aepjen

Zeedijk 1

✆ 626 8401

Trams 4, 9, 14, 16, 20, 24 and 25

Open: daily from 1500

This bar buzzes on a Saturday night when musicians play and the customers sing – you'll be hard-pressed to reach the bar. It's worth seeing for the building alone, as it's the oldest wooden house in Amsterdam.

Maximiliaan 18

Kloveniersburgwal 6–8

✆ 624 2778

Trams 4, 9, 14, 16, 20, 24 and 25

Open: daily from 1200

This terrific and lively brew-pub on several levels has an extensive list of beers, not just the ones brewed on the premises. If you're interested in seeing how it's done, phone in advance to arrange for a brewery tour. There's a good selection of food available too.

VOC Café 19

Schreierstoren, Prins Hendrikkade 94

✆ 428 8291

Trams 4, 9, 14, 16, 20, 24 and 25

Open: daily from 1000

If you're becoming a *jenever* (gin) connoisseur then you must visit this intimate little place tucked into the **Schreierstoren tower**, as it makes its own from an age-old recipe. Many liqueurs and beers are available too, with regular music and two canalside terraces. It's a great place to relax for a few hours.

THE OLD SIDE AND THE DAM
Shops, markets and picnic sites

Shops

De Bierkoning ⓴

Paleisstraat 125

Ø 625 2336

Ⓣ Trams 1, 2, 5, 13, 14, 16, 17, 20, 24 and 25

Open: Tue–Sat from 1100, Mon from 1300

Its neighbour the Royal Palace inspires the Beer King's regal name, but with about 850 beers claimed to be stocked, it can justify the claim. Specialist beer glasses are sold too, to go with the many Belgian beers, each of which has its own unique style of glass.

Geels & Co ㉑

Warmoesstraat 67

Ø 624 0683

Ⓣ Trams 4, 9, 14, 16, 20, 24 and 25

Open: Mon–Sat from 0900

This specialist tea and coffeeshop has loose beans, ground beans, herbal teas, China and Indian teas, and dozens of other varieties besides, as well as teapots and coffee mugs and percolators. Upstairs is a small museum open on Tuesday, Friday and Saturday afternoons only.

Jacob Hooy & Co ㉒

Kloveniersburgwal 10–12

Ø 624 3041

Ⓜ Metro to Nieuwmarkt or trams 4, 9, 14, 16, 20, 24 and 25

Open: Tue–Sat from 0830, Mon from 1000

Worth visiting for historical reasons alone, this apothecary opened in 1743 and is still going strong, with food lovers interested in its range of over 500 herbs and spices, 30 teas and a range of health foods. There are also cosmetics and homeopathic remedies available too.

Loekie ㉓

Prinsengracht 705a

Ø 624 4230

Ⓣ Trams 1, 2 and 5

Open: Mon–Sat from 0900

A sandwich shop may not sound like a culinary experience, but visit Loekie and you might change your mind. The finest of ingredients, such as parma ham or smoked salmon, can be combined with the finest of

▲ Jacob Hooy & Co

breads, such as ciabatta or a baguette, to produce a wonderful lunch or snack. Wines and other foodstuffs are for sale as well.

Oriental Commodities 24

Nieuwmarkt 27

✆ 638 6181

◉ Metro to Nieuwmarkt or trams 4, 9, 14, 16, 20, 24 and 25

Open: Mon–Sat from 0900

If you want to buy a wok then this huge Chinese supermarket on the edge of Chinatown is the place to do it. This is where many of the restaurants buy their sauces and other kitchen essentials, so if you are a fan of Chinese food spend some time browsing in here.

Wout Arxhoek 25

Damstraat 19

✆ 622 9118

◉ Trams 4, 9, 14, 16, 24 and 25

Open: Mon–Sat from 0900

This fantastic cheese shop right in the city centre is bright and clean with over 250 varieties of cheese, many of them Dutch, putting the lie to the fact that only Edam and Gouda are made in Holland.

Markets

Nieuwmarkt Market 26

Nieuwmarkt

▲ Nieuwmarkt Market

◉ Metro to Nieuwmarkt

Open: Sat from 0900

In this cobbled market square you'll discover not the biggest market in Amsterdam but one of the oldest. Foodies will find stalls selling organic produce, fruit, vegetables, bread and cheeses, amongst other things.

Family eating

Catering for all ages

Eating out with children is as easy and relaxed as anything else is in Amsterdam. For the fussy youngsters who want only what they can get back at home, there are numerous familiar fast food outlets such as **McDonald's**, **Burger King** and **Pizza Express**. Cafés and restaurants welcome children, and they are also allowed in bars and other places where alcohol is served, provided that they don't drink any and can behave themselves reasonably well.

If it's burger bars and similar places you're looking for, then there are plenty along **Damrak** as you walk away from the **Centraal Station**, and another stretch at the southern end of **Nieuwendijk**. There are plenty of stalls selling street snacks too, and few children will complain about the passion the Dutch have for chips,

usually dipped in mayonnaise as they do in Belgium. In these places are also numerous kiosks selling filled rolls and hot slices of apple pie, although the Dutch liking for raw herrings may not appeal quite so much to some children.

In addition, there are many places which go out of their way to cater for children, the best of these being the **Pancake Bakery** (*Prinsengracht 191; ✆ 625 1333;* ⚉ *trams 13, 17 and 20; open: daily from 1200;* 💳 💳 *American Express;* ⚉) most children like pancakes anyway, and this is one of the best places in the city to try them. There's an inventive array of over 70 varieties, from Cajun chicken to syrups and various ice cream flavours … with added liqueurs for the adult palate. There are separate children's menus and

children's chairs, as well as toys to play with and a general atmosphere of relaxed fun.

The best experience of all, though, for both adults and children, will require booking well in advance due to the limited size, restricted opening times, the great demand, the fantastic value for money and the unique nature of the enterprise. This is the **KinderKookKafé** (*Oudezijds Achterburgwal 193; ∅ 625 3257;* ● *trams 4, 9, 14, 16, 24 and 25; open: Sat dinner and Sun mid-afternoon but times vary so ring to check; reservations essential; no credit cards accepted;* ●).

At the KinderKookKafé children run the show. Children greet you when you arrive and show you to your table, they wait at table, they bring the bills, do the cooking and washing-up behind the scenes, and even run the bar and will bring you a bottle of the house white. Visiting children can volunteer to help if they wish, but you must arrange this in advance as the demand is high. Language needn't be a barrier as there are supervisors and even young Dutch children speak English and usually one other language. Children must be at least eight years of age to help with Saturday dinner, or five years and over for Sunday afternoon tea. Preparation for Saturday nights begins at about 1530, so be prepared for that if you want to be cooked for by your children.

> **Children greet you when you arrive and show you to your table, they wait at table, cook and bring the bills.**

The decoration is fun – rather like being in a box of liquorice allsorts – and the tables and chairs are all scaled-down in size. A charming touch is that the day's dishes, which are chalked on a blackboard, incorporate the names of the creators, so you may order Tom's curry or Marie's tiramisu (making it easy to give your compliments to the chef). Curries and other exotic dishes are common on the menu as this reflects the ethnic mix of the city and of the children who cook here, so Indonesian food is very common, but so are Surinamese, Indian, African, Spanish and many other cuisines besides – a splendid idea. Sunday afternoons are limited to coffee, tea, cakes, pastries and biscuits.

On top of the fun and the quality, which is obviously variable but generally good, the prices are usually bargains, with a sliding scale of lower prices depending on the age of the children … and children who cook get a discount.

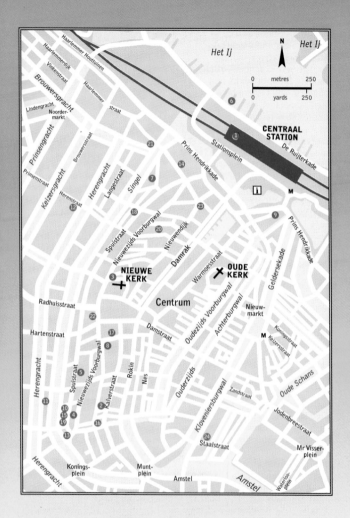

The New Side

The western half of the old city centre does have many modern buildings but plenty of historical interest too. For the food and drink lover it also houses some great city restaurants and brown bars, definitely the place to head if you like your nights lively.

THE NEW SIDE
Restaurants

1er Class ❶

Centraal Station, Line 2B

✆ 623 0131

🚊 Any tram to Centraal Station

Open: daily from 1700

Reservations recommended

All credit cards accepted

French

💶💶

Not many train station restaurants receive rave reviews, but this brasserie with its art-nouveau interior wins on both décor and creative French cuisine, although you can just call in and have a coffee or a beer if you prefer.

Begijntje ❷

Begijnesteeg 6–8

✆ 624 0528

🚊 Trams 1, 2 and 5

Open: daily for dinner

Reservations essential

All credit cards accepted

French-Dutch

💶💶

Set in a lovely former coach house, the Begijntje takes a French approach of offering a fixed menu each evening, so vegetarians and fussy eaters had better check in advance. The food combines Dutch traditions with French flair.

Crignon Culinaire ❸

Gravenstraat 28

✆ 624 6428

🚊 Trams 1, 2, 4, 5, 9, 14, 16, 20, 24 and 25

Open: Tue–Sat for dinner

Reservations essential

No credit cards accepted

French

💶

This small and cheerful place specialises in cheese dishes generally, and fondue in particular – hardly surprising as it's a cheese shop during the day! There are meat and fish dishes too, with

▲ The Supper Club

a French touch, and prices are inexpensive.

Haesje Claes ④

Spuistraat 273–75

∅ 624 9998

🚊 Trams 1, 2 and 5

Open: daily from noon

Reservations recommended

All credit cards accepted

Dutch

💶💶

Old wood and Delft crockery on the walls create the cosy setting of this Dutch restaurant in a 16th-century building. The food is moderately priced, unless you go for the caviar. Traditional dishes include *hutspot*, a beef stew.

Lucius ⑤

Spuistraat 247

∅ 624 1831

🚊 Trams 1, 2, 5, 13 and 17

Open: Mon–Sat dinner

Reservations recommended

All credit cards accepted

Seafood

💶💶💶

One of the city's most popular fish restaurants, established 25 years ago, Lucius imports fish from all over the world, not just the more common North Sea types. Expect lobster, oysters, mussels, salmon, John Dory, plaice, Dover sole and

many others, cooked any way you wish.

Pier 10 ⑥

De Ruijterkade, Steiger 10	
✆ 624 8276	
🚊 Any tram to Centraal Station	
Open: daily dinner only	
Reservations essential	
All credit cards accepted	
International	
❸❸❸	

Two rooms at the end of a pier behind Centraal Station afford great views over the water, so reserve in advance and ask for a good table in the glass room. The creative cuisine includes duck breast in grapefruit *confit*, and chocolate mousse with a passion fruit coulis.

De Silveren Spiegel ⑦

Kattengat 4–6	
✆ 624 6589	
🚊 Trams 1, 2, 5, 13, 17 and 20	
Open: daily for dinner, lunch by advance reservation	
Reservations recommended	
💳 💳 American Express	
Dutch-French	
❸❸❸	

Two 1614 houses form the relaxed and intimate setting for this favourite Amsterdam haunt, with its bar and series of dining rooms. Dutch lamb is a tradition and baked sole fillets with wild spinach another option.

The Supper Club ⑧

Jonge Roelensteeg 21	
✆ 638 0513	
🚊 Trams 1, 2, 5, 13 and 17	
Open: daily for dinner	
Reservations essential	
All credit cards accepted	
International	
❸❸	

There is nowhere quite like the Supper Club, which turns eating into an art experience. The décor changes with the fixed menus, so you may be lounging around in Arabian style on one visit or be in downtown Naples the next.

Vermeer ⑨

Prins Hendrikkade 59–72	
✆ 556 4885	
🚊 Any tram to Centraal Station	
Open: daily for dinner	
Reservations essential	
All credit cards accepted	
International	
❸❸❸	

Edwin Kats is a star Amsterdam chef, renowned for dishes such as pan-fried monkfish with mushrooms and a herb risotto. This luxury restaurant in two converted grand houses, with their plush armchairs and carpets, provides the perfect setting in which to enjoy his creations.

D'Vijff Vlieghen ⑩

Spuistraat 294–302	
✆ 624 8369	
🚊 Trams 1, 2, 5, 13, 17 and 20	
Open: daily for dinner	
Reservations recommended	
All credit cards accepted	
Dutch	
❸❸	

'The Five Flies' is named after the five canal houses it occupies, with its panelled Dutch interior including a **Rembrandt Room** with original etchings. The chef's nouvelle cuisine approach includes stuffed fillet of rabbit wrapped in gammon.

THE NEW SIDE
Bars, cafés and pubs

De Admiraal ⑪

Herengracht 319

✆ 625 4334

🚊 Trams 1, 2 and 5

Open: daily from 1700

€

This popular canalside bar starts late and finishes late. It specialises in liqueurs and *jenevers* (gins) but offers plenty of other drinking options too and one of the better bar menus in the city, including full meals, to accompany the booze.

De Beiaard ⑬

Spui 30

✆ 622 5110

🚊 Trams 1, 2 and 5

Open: daily from 1100

€

With a pleasant terrace overlooking the street, this café-bar is a congenial place with a superior food menu to many, though the main attraction is its range of over 70 bottled beers, including excellent Belgian brews.

The Blarney Stone ⑭

Nieuwendijk 29

✆ 623 3830

🚊 Trams 1, 2, 5, 13, 17 and 20

Open: daily from 1000

€

Irish pubs are as popular in Amsterdam as in many other cities, and there's a whole host to choose from. This central bar is definitely for those who like a raucous time, as it's quite small and basic and is usually packed.

Café Dante ⑮

Spuistraat 320

✆ 638 8839

🚊 Trams 1 and 5

Open: daily from 1100

€

Funky city bar that looks like any other from the outside, but inside turns into an art gallery too, with changing displays around the bar and also on the upstairs balconied seating area. The beer's good too!

Café Esprit ⑯

Spui 10a

✆ 622 4967

🚊 Trams 1, 2, 4, 5, 9, 14, 16, 20, 24 and 25

Open: from 1000, closed Tue and Sun

€

There's seating outside and a chic interior inside, rather as you'd expect from a café owned by a fashion store. Snack on salads and rolls, and coffee or wine are all on offer, or choose from the full menu of equally chic food with a healthy Californian slant.

Café Luxembourg ⑱

Spuistraat 22–4

✆ 620 6264

🚊 Trams 1, 2, 5, 13, 17 and 20

Open: daily from 0900, food from 1000

€ €

This very smart and long-established café is popular with the well-heeled set and serves snacks and main dishes, with *dim sum*, such as the *dim sum*, prepared for them by Amsterdam's restaurants. That said, it's worth visiting if you only have a coffee and linger over one of the international newspapers provided.

De Jonge Roel ⑰

Jonge Roelensteeg 4

✆ 421 7521

🚊 Trams 1, 2, 5, 13, 14, 17 and 20

Open: Mon–Fri from 1600, Sat–Sun from 1400

€

This began life as the Netherlands Beer Café, and it is another Amsterdam temple for the beer drinker, with a vast range of bottled and draught beers, including many Dutch ones to rival those of their Belgian neighbours.

De Stil 🔞

Spuistraat 326

✆ 620 1349

🚊 Trams 1, 2 and 5

Open: daily from 1000

€

The name tells you that this is no ordinary bar, but a haven for whisky-drinkers with its range of over 150 from Scotland, Ireland, the USA and anywhere else they make it. Look for the regular customers' private bottles kept on the shelves.

't Arendnest 🔢

Herengracht 90

✆ 622 5110

🚊 Trams 1, 2, 5, 13, 14, 17 and 20

Open: Tue–Thu 1500–0100, Fri 1500–0200, Sat 1400–0200, Sun 1400–2200

€

With a pleasant terrace overlooking the street, this bar is a congenial place with a better food menu than many, though the main attraction is its enormous range of Dutch beers from 75 different breweries.

De Wildeman 🔢

Nieuwezijds Kolk 3

✆ 638 2348

🚊 Trams 4, 9, 14, 16, 20, 24 and 25

Open: Mon–Sat from 1200, Sun from 1400

€

Any beer lovers should make a pilgrimage to this lively bar, with its changing range of 18 draught beers from all over the world, and a few hundred bottled beers too. In some countries this would be an alcoholics' dive, but in Amsterdam it's fun.

▲ Private whisky lockers at De Stil

THE NEW SIDE
Shops, markets and picnic sites

Shops

Chabrol 21

Haarlemmerstraat 7

✆ 622 2781

🚊 Trams 1, 2 and 5

Open: Mon–Sat from 0900, Sun from 1200

Lovely bright and well-stocked wine shop, with wines from all over the globe at very reasonable prices and a knowledgeable and helpful staff. Wine-tastings are organised too, which might coincide with your visit.

MAARTEN VAN CAULIL

Food Plaza 22

Nieuwezijds Voorburgwal

🚊 Trams 1, 2, 5, 13, 14, 16, 17, 20, 24 and 25

Open: daily from 0900

Next door to the Magna Plaza is the Food Plaza, and this is the place to head if you want to prepare a quick picnic lunch or if you are self-catering. Most of the ground floor comprises a huge supermarket, while around the edges

▲ Wines at Chabrol

▲ Magna Plaza

are several stalls selling snacks and fast foods, or salads, and there is also a fishmonger. The basement is given over to a large branch of the **Gall and Gall** wine merchants, in a suitably up-market cellar setting.

H P de Vreng en Zonen 23

Nieuwendijk 75

✆ 624 4581

Ⓣ Trams 1, 2, 5, 13, 17 and 20

Open: Mon–Sat from 0900

This is a terrific retail outlet for a distillery that makes traditional Dutch liqueurs and gins, and sells a vast range of others too, along with glasses, spirits and wines. It has a collection of 15,000 miniature bottles stored around the old beams – they're worth seeing even if you buy nothing.

Magna Plaza 22

Nieuwezijds Voorburgwal

Ⓣ Trams 1, 2, 5, 13, 14, 16, 17, 20, 24 and 25

Open: daily from 0900

The Magna Plaza shopping centre is just across from the Royal Palace and its ornate exterior may lead you to believe it was once part of the palace itself, but in fact it was built in 1899 to house the post office. Its five floors mainly contain high street and designer clothes shops, but there is a small and well-stocked cheese shop just inside the entrance, a pleasant brasserie on the ground floor and a busy café on the top floor.

Puccini Bomboni 24

Staalstraat 17

✆ 626 5474

Ⓜ Metro to Waterlooplein or trams 9, 14 and 20

Open: Tue–Sat from 0900

A patisserie that rivals those in Paris, serving up not only good home-baked bread but also sumptuous cake creations and elaborate desserts involving lots of chocolate, cream and strawberries.

Business dining

Doing business in style

Amsterdam may not have the same wide choice of top-notch eating places when compared to Paris, London or New York, but if you want to impress someone over a business lunch or dinner – or simply want to eat well – there are enough restaurants that combine excellent cooking with a sophisticated atmosphere.

One of the best options in the city is **Christophe'** (*Leliegracht 46; Ø 625 0807;* 🔘 *trams 13, 14, 17 and 20; open: Tue–Sat dinner; reservations essential; all credit cards accepted; French;* ❶❷❸). Christophe was born in Algeria and has worked at the Ritz in Paris, and for several top

restaurants in the USA, before setting up his own place in Amsterdam in 1987. He won his first Michelin star in 1989 and has kept it ever since.

The cooking stays true to Christophe's Mediterranean roots, but is influenced by his enthusiasm for travelling. There is a fixed-price menu and a 'Petit Menu', as well as à la carte. One recent fixed-price menu comprised a fondant of aubergine with cumin and a fresh herb salad; a 'Nage' of sea scallops and shrimp with saffron and orange; duck 'shepherd's pie' with shiitake mushrooms and black truffle; and caramelised pear on a short pastry crust.

The service is as impeccable as you would expect from a Michelin-starred restaurant – friendly without being fawning – and the décor is light and elegant. Business diners will find that the tables are well-spaced, so there's no risk of anyone eavesdropping on important deals, and for larger dinners there is also the 'Garden Room', just off the main restaurant, which seats from 6 to 14 people, but you need to book well in advance.

While Christophe' would suit informal business dinners, for a more serious rendezvous you might consider **Dorrius** (*Nieuwezijds Voorburgwal 5; Ø 620 0500;* 🔘 *trams 1, 2, 5, 13, 17 and 20; open: daily from*

▲ Excelsior

1200; reservations essential; all credit cards accepted; Dutch; ❶❷❸), with its hushed atmosphere beneath ancient beamed ceilings. Part of the **Crowne Plaza Hotel**, Dorrius occupies adjacent canal houses as it has done for the last hundred years. It offers a selection of 'Dorrius Classics', old Dutch recipes that it has been making for decades, such as a hunter's stew or braised beef with red cabbage. Alongside these are newer recipes including fried pikeperch with raspberry sauce.

Sitting somewhere in-between the tradition of Dorrius and the innovation of Christophe' is one of the most famous names in Amsterdam, **Excelsior** (*Hôtel de l'Europe, Nieuwe Doelenstraat 2–8; ✆ 531 1777;* ❶ *trams 4, 9, 16, 20, 24 and 25; open: Sun–Fri lunch and dinner and Sat dinner; reservations essential; all credit cards accepted; International;* ❶❷❸). This is where the most successful businessmen mingle with royalty and movie and media stars. The chandeliered dining room has picture windows overlooking the Amstel, and the formality is reflected in the fact that it is one of the few places in Amsterdam where men must wear a jacket.

Less formal is the cooking, which combines tradition with modern invention. Smoked eel with dill is an established Dutch starter, while main courses might include fillet of veal with leek sauce. The consistency of the

▲ Chef at Mangerie de Kersentuin

cooking has also earned the Excelsior the coveted Michelin star. If Michelin is your guideline then don't ignore the two stars awarded to **La Rive** (*see page 80*).

Another excellent hotel restaurant is at the **Bilderberg Garden Hotel** in the south side of the city – **Mangerie de Kersentuin** (*Dijsselhofplantsoen 7; ✆ 664 2121;* ❶ *tram 16; open: Mon–Fri 1200–1400, 1800–2300, Sat 1000–2300; reservations recommended; all credit cards accepted; International;* ❶❷❸). The dining room alone is enough to impress the most jaded visitor, with its floor-to-ceiling windows looking out on to the street on one side, and into the kitchen on the other. *Kersentuin* means 'Cherry Orchard', and the cherry-red colouring, combined with lots of gleaming brass, creates one of the city's best dining rooms. Fortunately the food lives up to the surroundings, with dishes reading like a poem: 'lamb fillet prepared in goose fat with creamy salsifies, and coriander-scented vanilla sauce'. If that doesn't keep business diners happy, nothing will.

> **Smoked eel with dill is an established Dutch starter, while main courses might include fillet of veal with leek sauce.**

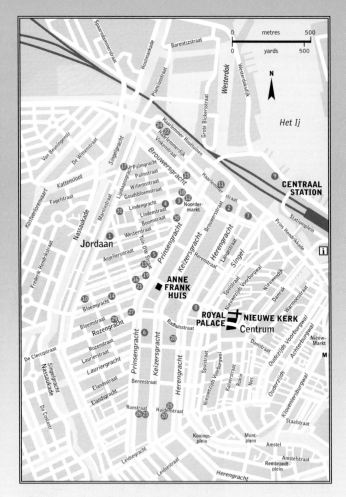

Jordaan and the Northern Canals

To the east of the city centre is the Jordaan, one of the most delight-ful areas of Amsterdam. Its quiet streets and canals are mainly residential, and it's a fashionable place to live, but here too are some of the more sophisticated restaurants and atmospheric old brown bars in which to while away many an hour.

Albatros ❶

Westerstraat 264	
✆ 627 9932	
🚋 Tram 10	
Open: Thu–Tue for dinner	
Reservations recommended	
All credit cards accepted	
Seafood	
€€	

A jaunty blue-and-white nautical décor and an affable owner greet you in this casual Jordaan fish specialist restaurant. Whatever is fresh will be on the menu, and you can expect to have the choice of sole, plaice, salmon and tuna steaks.

De Belhamel ❷

Brouwersgracht 60	
✆ 622 1095	
🚋 Trams 1, 2, 5, 13, 17 and 20	
Open: daily for dinner	
Reservations recommended	
All credit cards accepted	
French-Dutch	
€€	

Casual and intimate restaurant on two levels, at the junction of two canals. The tables are quite packed in, which people love as it creates a really friendly and intimate ambience. Creative dishes include beef tenderloin in a Madeira sauce.

Bordewijk ❸

Noordermarkt 7	
✆ 624 3899	
🚋 Tram 3 or buses 18 and 22	
Open: Tue–Sun for dinner	
Reservations recommended	
💳 💳 American Express	
French-Fusion	
€€	

▲ Claes Claesz

At this highly rated restaurant with white walls and plenty of plants, the French cuisine also has Italian and Asian touches, so on the menu sushi sits alongside pigeon cooked in the style of Bresse.

Caffé Toscanini ④

Lindengracht 75

✆ 623 2813

🚊 Trams 3 and 10 or buses 18 and 22

Open: daily for dinner

Reservations recommended

All credit cards accepted

Italian

💰💰

There's a great atmosphere and delicious southern Italian food in this simply decorated place. In an open kitchen a surprisingly small number of chefs

prepare sublime dishes such as deep-fried stuffed olives and mouth-watering *panna cotta*.

Claes Claesz ⑤

Egelantiersstraat 24–6

✆ 625 5306

🚊 Trams 7, 10, 17 and 20

Open: Tue–Sun dinner only

Reservations recommended

💳💳💳

Dutch

●●

One of the best places in the area for sampling Dutch food, the restaurant building dates from 1600 but the food trend is emphatically modern and is served in a busy but amiable atmosphere, usually with live music.

De Goudsbloem ⑥

Hotel Pulitzer, Prinsengracht 315–31

∅ 523 5283

🚋 Trams 13, 14, 17 and 20

Open: daily for dinner

Reservations recommended

All credit cards accepted

French

●●●

Much better than the average hotel restaurant, this sophisticated yet relaxed place offers superb French cooking, such as a plate of smoked salmon served in goose gravy. It boasts one of the city's – if not Europe's – best wine cellars too.

Himalaya ⑦

Haarlemmerstraat 11

∅ 622 3776

🚋 Trams 1, 2, 5, 13, 17 and 20

Open: daily for dinner

Reservations unnecessary

All credit cards accepted

Indian

●

A simple and unpretentious restaurant with welcoming staff which serves better than average food at lower than

average prices. Balti and tandoori dishes feature, and the staff will tailor the spices to suit your palate.

Leg Af ⑧

Oude Leliestraat 9

∅ 624 6700

🚋 Trams 1, 2, 5, 13, 14, 17 and 20

Open: daily for dinner

Reservations unnecessary

No credit cards accepted

Fusion

●

One of Amsterdam's popular fondue places, Leg Af is very different as it prepares international styles such as a British cheddar and cider fondue, and at weekends adds sushi and *sashimi* dishes to the menu.

Osaka ⑨

12th Floor, Het Havengebouw, De Ruijterkade 7

∅ 638 9833

🚋 Any tram to Centraal Station

Open: Mon–Fri from 1200, Sat–Sun from 1700

Reservations recommended

All credit cards accepted

Japanese

●●●

Probably the best Japanese food in town, and certainly the best views, though if you choose the *tepanyaki* grill section with the fast-working chefs you stare out over Centraal Station rather than the harbour.

Vliegende Schotel ⑩

Nieuwe Leliestraat 162

∅ 625 2041

🚋 Trams 13, 14, 17 and 20

Open: daily in summer from 1300, in winter from 1700

Reservations not allowed

No credit cards accepted

Vegetarian

●

The 'Flying Saucer' is a café-cum-casual restaurant with great character, as locals join each other at tables with spare chairs, and the food, such as the vegetarian *rijsttafel*, is substantial and cheap. It's not licensed to sell alcohol.

JORDAAN AND THE NORTHERN CANALS
Bars, cafés and pubs

Café du Lac

Haarlemmerstraat 118

⌀ 624 4265

🚌 Buses 18 and 22

Open: Mon–Fri from 1600,
Sat–Sun from 1400

💶💶

One of Amsterdam's
best and best-loved
Grand Cafés, with its
rather bizarre, old-fash-
ioned and eccentric
interior, music at the
weekend, a lovely rear
terrace and the option
to have just drinks or
sample something from
the Mediterranean
menu.

Café Papeneiland

Prinsengracht 2

⌀ 624 1989

🚌 Buses 18 and 22

Open: daily from 1100

💶

Established in 1642, this
is one of the oldest
brown bars in the city
and it oozes age and
conviviality with its
ancient stove, canalside
setting, cheerful Delft
tiles and even more
cheerful customers.

Café 't Smalle

Egelantiersgracht 12

⌀ 623 9617

🚊 Trams 3, 5, 12 and 24

Open: daily from 1100

💶

Originally founded in
1786 as a distillery, one
wonders how much
alcohol has been brewed
and, more recently,
drunk in this brown bar
which, despite its age
and recent restoration to
its 18th-century origins,
still attracts a fairly
young crowd of
drinkers.

Nieuwe Lelie

Nieuwe Leliestraat 83

⌀ 622 5493

🚊 Trams 10, 13, 14, 17
and 20

Open: Mon–Sat from 1400,
Sun from 1600

💶

One of Amsterdam's
old-fashioned brown
bars in the heart of the
Jordaan, with split-level
seating and a relaxed
atmosphere where locals
come to chat and play
chess and few visitors
venture.

Oranjerie

Binnen Oranjestraat 15

⌀ 623 4611

 Tram 3 or buses 18 and 22

Open: Mon–Fri from 1600, Sat from 1200, Sun from 1300

Another laid-back brown bar in the Jordaan, but less busy than many as it's tucked away slightly on a side street, so preferred by those who want to chat and relax rather than spend a rowdy evening drinking heavily.

De Reiger

Nieuwe Leliestraat 34

☏ 624 7426

 Trams 10, 13, 14, 17 and 20

Open: daily from 1100, hot meals from 1800

This small corner bar in the Jordaan serves beer and cold snacks during the day, such as a smoked chicken and mustard mayonnaise

sandwich, and more substantial fare in the evening when it gets packed quickly due to its location and laid-back feel.

SAS

Marnixstraat 79

☏ 420 4075

 Trams 7, 10, 17 and 20

Open: daily from 1400

Bizarre but endearing bar, whose décor changes whenever the owner feels like it. Not a tourist in sight, but the canalside seating at the rear is very much what Amsterdam is about, and good food is available too.

Thijssen

Brouwersgracht 107

☏ 623 8994

 Tram 3

Open: Sun–Fri from 0930, Sat from 0700

Well-loved Jordaan brown bar on a canal-side corner, with plenty of outdoor seating, which is usually filled with locals in animated conversation, especially on a Saturday with two markets taking place close by.

Twee Zwaanties

Prinsengracht 114

☏ 625 2729

 Trams 13, 14, 17 and 20

Open: Mon–Sat from 2000, Sun from 1500

Definitely one for the locals, though lucky tourists who wander in at night and catch the boisterous singing and accordion players will love it. The bar is small so you may have to stand or sit outside and listen.

JORDAAN AND THE NORTHERN CANALS
Shops, markets and picnic sites

Shops

Gimsel 20

Huidenstraat 19

✆ 624 8087

🔔 Trams 1, 2 and 5

Open: Mon from 1230, Tue–Fri from 0930, Sat from 0900

If you are into health foods then take a look at Gimsel, which has a good stock of organically grown fruit and vegetables, plus other foodstuffs such as cereals and cakes, as well as bread.

Glasgalerie Kuhler 21

Prinsengracht 134

✆ 638 0230

🔔 Trams 13, 14, 16 and 20

Open: Tue–Sat from 1200, first Sun of each month 1300–1600

There's a wonderful array of glassware here, whether you're looking for stylish wineglasses, elegant champagne flutes or chunky tumblers. Much of the work is original, signed by the artists, and there are also glass sculptures, flower vases, lampshades and other accoutrements.

J G Beune 22

Haarlemmerdijk 156–8

✆ 624 8356

🔔 Tram 3 or buses 18 and 22

Open: Mon–Sat from 0830

For a bakery that is over a century old, this shop keeps up well with the times, offering a service that will produce a cake topping copied digitally from a photograph. Sample the delicious cakes and pastries, and the freshly made loaves and rolls.

De Kaaskamer 23

Runstraat 7

✆ 623 3483

🔔 Trams 1, 2 and 5

Open: Tue–Fri from 1000, Sat from 0900

This bright cheese shop with an attractive exterior stocks about 200 cheeses from Holland, France, Belgium and elsewhere, which you could put together with some of the olives, pâtés, salads and other delicatessen items to produce a picnic. You can even buy a bottle of wine here too.

Mediterranee 24

Haarlemmerdijk 184

✆ 620 3550

🔔 Tram 3 or buses 18 and 22

Open: daily from 0800

This wonderful bakery sells a tempting variety of breads, all made on the premises but using traditions from the shores of the Mediterranean – mainly France and Morocco – as well as Dutch breads too.

Patisserie Pompadour 25

Huidenstraat 12

✆ 623 9554

🔔 Trams 1, 2, 5 and 7

Open: Tue–Fri from 0930, Sat from 0830

A Parisian-style pastry shop whose displays of chocolates and cakes made on the premises are inspired by the best of French, Belgian and Dutch styles and flavours, using the best quality ingredients. A small tearoom gives you space to relax or indulge yourself with pastries.

Paul Anne 26

Runstraat 25

✆ 623 5322

🔔 Trams 1, 2, 5, 7, 10 and 20

Open: Mon–Fri from 0845, Sat from 0900

This bakery-cum-health-food store bakes all its own bread from organic ingredients, though healthy doesn't mean boring as their range of cakes and pastries shows. A sourdough bread is one of their specialities, and you could combine it with cheese from the Kaaskamer shop along the street for a good picnic lunch.

Simon Levelt 27

Prinsengracht 180

✆ 624 0823

🚊 Trams 13, 14, 17 and 20

Open: Mon–Sat from 0830

A canalside tea and coffeeshop that dates back to 1839 and where the aroma will draw you in to smell and sample the range of goods. There are a few dozen coffees from all over the world, with bags of beans and pre-packed ground coffee, as well as all the accoutrements of coffee-making. Then there are over 100 types of tea, from India and Sri Lanka, from China and the Far East, and especially from the former Dutch colony of Indonesia. You can also buy attractive selection boxes which make good souvenirs or presents.

A Taste of Ireland 28

Herengracht 228

✆ 638 1642

🚊 Trams 13, 14, 17 and 20

Open: Mon from 1300, Tue–Fri from 1000, Sat from 1100

Not the usual Irish souvenir shop with Aran sweaters but one devoted to Irish food, with black and white pudding, bacon, biscuits, jam, honey, whiskies, beers and other tasty goodies.

Wegewijs 29

Rozengracht 32

✆ 624 4093

🚊 Trams 13, 14, 17 and 20

Open: Mon–Sat from 0830

If you want to know more about the wide variety of Dutch cheeses that exist, visit this shop that has been in the same family since the late 19th century. There are over a hundred Dutch cheeses in stock, any of which you can try, and the staff will tell you something about them. There are also a few dozen imported cheeses available too.

Markets

Boerenmarkt 30

Westerstraat/Noorderkerkstraat

🚊 Trams 3 and 10

Open: Sat from 1000

This excellent little organic farmers' market happens every Saturday until well into the afternoon in Noordermarkt, just a stroll away from the more commercial Lindengracht market. Here you'll find healthy-looking fruit and veg, mushrooms, cheeses, bread, spices and olive oils, plus a jovial, relaxed atmosphere.

Lindengracht Market 31

Lindengracht

🚊 Trams 3 and 10 or buses 18 and 22

Open: Sat from 1000

Big and busy street market that runs almost the whole length of Lindengracht, with clothes, CDs, books and other goods mixed up among the food and fast food stalls. Prices are cheaper than at the nearby Boerenmarkt, but you won't get the range of quality foods.

▲ Lindengracht Market

Brown bars

Home from home

All cities have their bars but only Amsterdam has its brown bars. The fact that they are sometimes also called brown cafés indicates that definitions don't matter too much here, and in Amsterdam you can get beer in a café just as easily as coffee in a bar. You can also get food in both places too – sometimes excellent, creative hot meals … and sometimes just a sandwich.

Brown bars get their name from the nicotine-stained walls that have been built up over the years, often over the centuries as the tradition of the brown bar goes back a few hundred years. Even so, new brown bars open all the time, so you are not automatically walking into history when you walk through the door, but a brown bar that doesn't have the right feel won't survive for very long. You might not be able to define it, but Amsterdammers know what it is.

Until you've experienced a brown bar in Amsterdam you would be forgiven for wondering just how one type of bar here can be different from others in other cities around the world. The answer is a Dutch word *gezellig*.

There is no direct translation of *gezellig*, but it's a mixture of feeling comfortable, feeling cosy, feeling friendly towards your fellow citizens and feeling at home, even if you're out in a bar. If you see a group of friends chatting around a table, that's *gezellig*. If a spontaneous singsong breaks out in a Dutch bar, that's *gezellig* too. And brown bars are very *gezellig*. It means they resemble the type of British pub which is all too rare now, with no pinball machines and fake antiques, but with regular customers and a friendly barman. If you add to this a feel of the American TV bar from *Cheers!* where the bonhomie is tangible and the mood convivial, then you start to get a picture of an Amsterdam brown bar.

Café de Druif (*see page 82*) is a small and homely place, opened in 1631 and whose name means 'The Grape'. In some places when a stranger walks into a bar, the stares are suspicious, like the stranger walking into the western saloon. But when a stranger walks into a bar like De Druif, the stares are merely curious and welcoming, wondering about the

▲ Café de Druif

adventurous visitor who has stumbled upon their little home from home. It is set back a little from the main Amsterdam waterfront, on a square that's alongside the start (or end) of the Herengracht canal, and close to a typical Dutch lock gate. It's the kind of place where, if you arrive in the early evening and the mood is just right, you will find yourself settling in for the night.

The same applies to most other brown bars, not least because they get so crowded that once you get in you may find it impossible to get out again. One such is an Amsterdam institution, the **Café Tabac** (*Brouwersgracht 101*; ✆ *622 6520*; ⊛ *trams 1, 2, 5, 13, 17 and 20; open: daily from 1130*). It stands at the junction of the Prinsengracht and Brouwersgracht canals, and seems to be busy whatever time of day or night it is. A few coveted tables stand outside, though the regulars spill over beyond these to enjoy the canalside views. Inside is a long, narrow room with a bar along one side, and the décor is nothing special but then that is part of the charm of most brown bars. They haven't been designed like modern bars, they have just evolved over the years. The Tabac serves *tapas* and other snacks, and a small range of hot meals, but you don't go there to dine, you go to enjoy what the Irish call the *craic*.

▲ Café de Druif

Gollem (*Raamsteeg 4*; ✆ *626 6645*; ⊛ *trams 1, 2 and 5; open: daily from 1600*) is one of the newer bars and was the first in the city to offer a really good range of beers. For many years the locals were perfectly happy to down their Amstels and Heinekens, till people discovered a new interest in beer, and Gollem began importing Belgian and other brews and stocking the best from Holland too. It has over 100 available, a true beer hunter's delight.

By contrast the **Hoppe** (*Spui 18–20*; ✆ *420 4420*; ⊛ *trams 1, 2, 4, 5, 9, 14, 16, 20, 24 and 25; open: daily from 0800*) is one of the oldest in Amsterdam, dating back to about 1670. Its tiny bar soon gets packed, but if you can make it inside then you're in for a real brown bar experience. You'll discover that health warnings don't seem to have done much to reduce the smoking habits of Amsterdam's citizens, so the brown bars will just carry on getting browner and browner ...

> **When a stranger walks into a bar, the stares are merely curious and welcoming, wondering about the adventurous visitor that has stumbled upon their little home from home.**

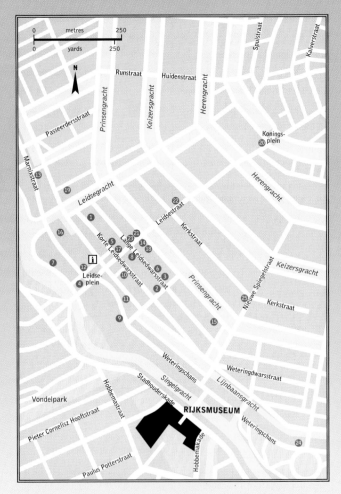

Leidseplein and the Central Canal Ring

The raucous Leidseplein is for those who like their bars and nightlife, and who enjoy crowds and music. It's the best area to sample some of the city's good ethnic restaurants, especially Indonesian and Indian, before or after a night on the town.

LEIDSEPLEIN AND THE CENTRAL CANAL RING
Restaurants

Akbar ❶

Korte Leidsedwarsstraat 15

✆ 624 2211

🚊 Trams 1, 2, 5, 6, 7, 10 and 20

Open: daily from 1700

Reservations unnecessary

All credit cards accepted

Indian

€€

In an area thronging with fast food and cheap food, Akbar is a reliable choice for its reasonably priced and tasty food, such as chicken tandoori, curried prawn dishes and many vegetarian options.

De Blauwe Hollander ❷

Leidsekruisstraat 28

✆ 623 3014

🚊 Trams 1, 2, 5, 6, 7, 10 and 20

Open: daily from 1700

Reservations unnecessary

No credit cards accepted

Dutch

€

An eating experience if you want a budget meal, with only four large communal tables where you will get basic dishes such as roast beef or fried chicken, with chips and salad or vegetables. A good find in this busy area.

Bojo ❸

Lange Leidsedwarsstraat 51

✆ 622 7434

🚊 Trams 1, 2 and 5

Open: Mon–Fri from 1600, Sat–Sun from 1200

Reservations unnecessary

No credit cards accepted

Indonesian

€

This is a cheap and cheerful Indonesian restaurant, in an area where there are plenty of poor-quality places. They serve the classic *rijsttafel* for two people, or try something different such as *cummi cummi*, which is squid.

Café Américain ❹

American Hotel, Leidskade 97

✆ 556 3000

🚊 Trams 1, 2, 5, 6, 7, 10 and 20

Open: daily from 1030, hot meals lunch and dinner

Reservations recommended

All credit cards accepted

International

€€€

Grand Café atmosphere with chandeliers and high ceilings and a wide menu that includes fresh fish such as monkfish or meat dishes like rack of Irish lamb. Alternatively, have a coffee and soak up the atmosphere.

De Oesterbar ❺

Leidseplein 10

✆ 623 2988

🚊 Trams 1, 2, 5, 6, 7, 10 and 20

Open: daily from 1200

Reservations unnecessary

All credit cards accepted

Seafood

€€–€€€

Book for the restaurant but take pot luck with the more casual downstairs tables. Oysters are a house speciality but there are plenty of fresh fish dishes too, including a mixed seafood plate of turbot, halibut and salmon.

Puri Mas ❻

Lange Leidsedwarsstraat 37–41

✆ 627 7627

🚊 Trams 1, 2 and 5

Open: daily from 1700

Reservations recommended

All credit cards accepted

Indonesian

€€

This haunt is rated by many as the city's best Indonesian restaurant, and it is certainly one of the more up-market ones. The menu is little different – expect *gado*

▲ Café Américain

gado and *rijsttafel* – but the quality is far superior to most other places.

De Smoeshaan **7**

Leidsekade 90	
⦶ 627 6966	
⊙ Trams 1, 2, 5, 6, 7, 10 and 20	
Open: café daily from 1100, restaurant Tue–Sat from 1730	
Reservations recommended	
⬤⬛ American Express	
French-Dutch	
⬤	

This popular place isn't haute cuisine but offers a range of good-value dishes in its upstairs restaurant, especially for vegetarians, while

downstairs is a busy café-bar where you can hang out, drink and snack.

Swaagat **8**

Lange Leidsedwarsstraat 76	
⦶ 638 4702	
⊙ Trams 1, 2 and 5	
Open: daily for dinner, and for lunch in summer	
Reservations unnecessary	
All credit cards accepted	
Indian	
⬤⬤	

A reliable choice in this neighbourhood of ethnic eating places, the Swaagat has a clean and pleasant décor with a good range of vegetarian dishes as well as the usual tandoori, balti

and biriyani fish and meat dishes too.

Teppan Yaki Hosokawa **9**

Max Euweplein 22	
⦶ 638 8086	
⊙ Trams 1, 2, 5, 6, 7, 10 and 20	
Open: daily from 1700	
Reservations unnecessary	
All credit cards accepted	
Japanese	
⬤⬤	

If you want to see how professional Japanese chefs work then you must come here, where your table will have a grill on it and you can watch the cook chopping and cooking with amazing dexterity.

't Swarte Schaep 🔟

Korte Leidsedwarsstraat 24

✆ 622 3021

🚊 Trams 1, 2, 5, 6, 7, 10 and 20

Open: daily from 1200

Reservations recommended

All credit cards accepted

Dutch

€€€

'The Black Sheep' seems just that, in its 17th-century home in the middle of brash Leidseplein, but the dark and cosy dining room offers simple but perfect Dutch cuisine, concentrating on the sea: grilled salmon, John Dory and many more.

▲ *Gado gado* at Puri Mas

LEIDSEPLEIN AND THE CENTRAL CANAL RING
Bars, cafés and pubs

De Balie ⑪

Kleine Gartmanplantsoen 10
✆ 553 5130
🚊 Trams 1, 2, 5, 6, 7, 10 and 20
Open: daily from 1100, Jul–Aug from 1200 only
€

The café-bar at **De Balie Theatre** is a great place for passing the time – appropriately enough, as it used to be a prison. The usual coffees and beers are augmented by some simple food, available upstairs.

Café Cox ⑫

Marnixstraat 429
✆ 620 7222
🚊 Trams 1, 2, 5, 6, 7, 10 and 20
Open: daily from 1000, hot dishes lunch and dinner
€ €

In the foyer of the **City Theatre**, the Cox is a lively meeting place if you just want a drink. There's a plush downstairs bar, but upstairs is also smart, with an airy restaurant serving French-Dutch cuisine.

Café de Koe ⑬

Marnixstraat 381
✆ 625 4482
🚊 Trams 7, 10 and 17
Open: Mon–Thu from 1600, Fri–Sun from 1500
€

An eccentric but endearing place in true Amsterdam fashion, the 'Cow Café' is decorated with a cow motif, and there are pool and pinball machines adding to the rowdy atmosphere, if that's what you want. Good-value food is available too.

Gary's Muffins ⑭

Prinsengracht 454
✆ 420 1452
🚊 Trams 1, 2 and 5
Open: Mon–Sat from 0830, Sun from 0900
€

There are several branches of Gary's Muffins in the city, and this is one of the busiest. They are hardly typical Dutch eating places, although the people who frequent the coffee-houses where soft drugs are available like them as they satisfy the subsequent craving for something sweet. You don't have to have had drugs to enjoy the bagels and cakes, though.

Lunchtime ⑮

Prinsengracht 560
✆ 627 2643
🚊 Trams 1, 2, 5, 6, 7, 10 and 20
Open: daily from 1000
€

This smart little basement café has friendly owners whose décor suggests a travelling past. The simple but tasty food on the menu includes sandwiches, soups, apple pies, fresh orange juice, coffees and a few light meals.

▲ Gary's Muffins

▲ Reynders

Melkweg/ Eat at Jo's 16

Marnixstraat 409

✆ 420 7469

🚊 Trams 1, 2, 5, 6, 7, 10 and 20

Open: Wed–Sun from 1400, hot meals from 1730

€

The Melkweg is an Amsterdam institution, combining bar, café, multimedia centre and a restaurant, which during the day is an independent operation called Eat at Jo's. Soup and sandwiches are served at lunch and in the afternoon, the evening menu offers one fish, one meat and one vegetarian option. A great place to hang out and find out what's on in the city.

Reynders 17

Leidseplein 6

✆ 623 4419

🚊 Trams 1, 2, 5, 6, 7, 10 and 20

Open: daily from 0900

€

An old-fashioned brown bar right on Leidseplein, where few such places remain amid the brash bars offering large-screen TVs and Happy Hour drinking. Here you can relax in more typical Amsterdam style, in what was once the literary centre of the area.

De Tap 18

Prinsengracht 478

✆ 622 9915

🚊 Trams 1, 2, 5, 6, 7, 10 and 20

Open: daily from 1600

€

Another good bolt-hole from the tourist traps around Leidseplein, this brown bar with its wood panelling and tiled floor has a relaxed Amsterdam feeling and a decent food menu too.

De Zotte Proeflokaal 19

Raamstratt 29

✆ 626 8694

🚊 Trams 1, 2, 5, 6, 7, 10 and 20

Open: daily from 0400

€

This bar-café specialises in Belgian beer, with hundreds of types, and at weekends hardly closes, shutting down at 0300 only to re-open an hour later. It also has a wide choice of liqueurs, and some snacks to go with it all.

LEIDSEPLEIN AND THE CENTRAL CANAL RING
Shops, markets and picnic sites

🚋 Trams 1, 2 and 5

Open: Mon–Sat from 1000, Sun from 1200

This is one of the busiest and most central branches of the supermarket chain which has almost 50 shops throughout the city. If you are not looking for gourmet fare but cheap foodstuffs, perhaps if you are self-catering with unadventurous children, then the Heijn

▲ Eichholtz

stores are your best bet for everyday items.

The Coffee Company 21

Leidsestraat 60
✆ 622 1519
🚋 Trams 1, 2 and 5
Open: Mon–Sat from 1000

This is a mix of coffee bar and retail shop, with a small selection of fresh beans and ground coffees for sale.

Eichholtz 22

Leidsestraat 48
✆ 622 0305
🚋 Trams 1, 2 and 5
Open: Tue–Sat from 0900, Sun from 1300, Mon from 1000

A venerable Amsterdam delicatessen, but with a strong emphasis on chocolates, cakes, biscuits and anything sweet. The shop imports produce from Britain and America, as well as selling an array of Dutch chocolates.

Errol Trumpie 23

Leidsestraat 46
✆ 624 0233
🚋 Trams 1, 2 and 5
Open: Mon–Sat from 0900

This place is worth seeking out if you want a relaxing cup of tea and a snack in the Leidseplein, as there is a small café attached to this patisserie, which also gives you a chance to sample the handmade pastries before buying some of them, or the handmade chocolates, from the shop.

▲ De Natuurwinkel

De Natuurwinkel 24

Weteringschans 133–7
✆ 638 4083
🚋 Trams 6, 7 and 10
Open: Mon–Sat from 0700, Sun from 1100

There are several branches of this health-food chain in the city, but this is the main one with everything for the healthy eater, from obvious choices such as fruit, vegetables, rice and bread, to a healthy choice of beer, wine and chocolates!

Volendammer Vishandel 25

Nieuwe Spiegelstraat 54
✆ 623 2962
🚋 Trams 1, 2 and 5
Open: Mon–Sat from 0900

You are not likely to be buying fresh fish unless you are self-catering in Amsterdam, but it is always interesting to see what is for sale in a well-stocked shop such as this. Remember what's fresh that day might end up on the restaurant menu that night.

Street food: chips and herrings

Eating on the hoof

Snacking in the street in Amsterdam might not initially seem like a tempting prospect, with the two favourite foods being chips and raw herring (separately, not together). However, once you start to look around there is a lot more variety available, thanks to the ethnic mix of the city. While it may not exactly be Bangkok or Hong Kong when it comes to street snacks, Amsterdam does have more to offer than just fried potatoes and uncooked fish.

To sample the best of the street food available from places such as Indonesia, Suriname and the Middle East, you need to visit the markets, especially the **Albert Cuypmarkt** (*see page 65*) and the **Dappermarkt** (*see page 84*). Here you'll be able to snack on dishes such as *falafel*, roast chicken with satay sauce or just plain roast chicken done on a vast rotisserie so that the juice is dripping and the smell almost irresistible.

You might find such stalls popping up almost anywhere in the city, but they are nowhere near as common as the ubiquitous stalls selling portions of chips. Known elsewhere as French fries, here in Amsterdam they are *Vlaamse frites*, or **Flemish fries**. Like their Belgian neighbours (but few other nations), the Dutch like to eat these accompanied by mayonnaise, but the stalls that sell them offer a whole host of dips to go with them, including mustard, tomato ketchup, peanut sauce, a slightly peppery goulash sauce and curry sauce.

Other options you'll see on the menus at the *Vlaamse frites* stalls and fast food shop counters include *kroketten* and *fricandel*. The latter is a **thin sausage** like a Frankfurter, while *kroketten* are tastier **croquettes**. They are made of minced meat mixed with pepper and spices, then covered in breadcrumbs and deep-fried in batter. They are not exactly a health-conscious option, but they can be incredibly moreish if you are in the mood. So too are *bitterballen*, which are **deep-fried cheese croquettes**, and *frikadellen*, which are **spicy meatballs** similar to *kroketten* but not deep-fried.

You'll see takeaway places everywhere, including

McDonald's, Burger King and several pizza chains, and there is also a Dutch chain called **FEBO** where you can buy *Vlaamse frites* with their various accompaniments as well as fried chicken, burgers and other international fast food fuel. There are also a number of Indonesian fast food places, where you might get a more unusual quick treat, and you'll see many places with 'Falafel' signs outside them too.

If you want a quick street snack but are not a chips and burgers person, head for one of the shops advertising *belegde broodje*, or **filled rolls**. These are often bread shops, so the bread is fresh and you'll have a choice of types, and the *belegde broodje* counter will be a miniature delicatessen with a whole array of fillings laid out for your inspection, including salads, tuna, smoked salmon, cheeses, cold meats and many other delights. Another sandwich snack you will often see advertised is a *uitsmijter*, which is an **open sandwich** with a few layers of meat and a fried egg on top.

Amsterdam does have more to offer than just fried potatoes and uncooked fish.

If you've a craving for something sweet then there are also stalls and takeaways which sell **pancakes** and **waffles**, and many of the fast food places include these on the menu too. Pancakes can have fillings that are sweet, spicy or savoury, and waffles usually come smothered in maple syrup.

Finally there is the most popular street snack of all: *harring*. The little **herrings** from the North Sea are marinated and sold in a roll with onions and cucumber pickle, although some people prefer to eat just the herring and let it slip down the throat like an oyster. May and June see the new herring catch, when the fish are said to be at their best and referred to as *nieuwe harring*, new herrings. The stalls which sell herrings may also well have other seafood snacks, so take a look at what's on offer. These could include smoked eel, oysters and mussels, mackerel and other fishes which may be smoked, deep-fried or pickled.

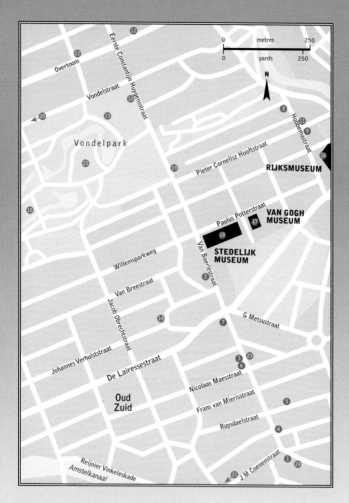

The Museum Quarter

Most visitors come here in the day to take in the Rijksmuseum and the Van Gogh Museum, with the Film Museum and Stedelijk Museum also nearby. Check the eating options to make sure you have a good lunch, and allow time to look at some of the up-market specialist food shops too.

THE MUSEUM QUARTER
Restaurants

Beddington's ❶

Roelof Hartstraat 6–8

✆ 676 5201

🚊 Trams 3, 5, 12, 20 and 24

Open: Tue–Fri lunch and dinner, Mon and Sat dinner only

Reservations recommended

All credit cards accepted

French-Fusion

💳💳

The chic artist-designed décor serves as a stylish backdrop to Jean Beddington's inventive French cooking influenced by his Eastern travels. Smoked eel terrine is a signature dish, as is Sea Devil tandoori.

Bodega Keyzer ❷

Van Baerlestraat 96

✆ 671 1441

🚊 Trams 2, 3, 5, 12, 16 and 20

Open: Mon–Sat from 0900, Sun from 1100

Reservations unnecessary

All credit cards accepted

International

💳💳💳

There's a dark and aged interior in this restaurant that was established in 1903, next to the **Concertgebouw**. It therefore attracts a respectable and well-heeled clientele, and its sole meunière dish has been around almost as long as the restaurant itself.

Brasserie van Baerle ❸

Van Baerlestraat 158

✆ 679 1532

🚊 Trams 2, 3, 5, 12 and 20

Open: Mon–Fri from 1200, Sun from 1000

Reservations recommended

💳💳 American Express

International

💳💳

A fashionable place in a century-old town house that's light and airy, proving popular with the local media set. Young chefs fuse brasserie food with international nouvelle cuisine, so oriental salads sit alongside grilled tuna steaks.

Café-Restaurant Wildschut ❹

Roelof Hartplein 1–3

✆ 676 8220

🚊 Trams 3, 5, 12, 20 and 24

Open: Mon–Fri from 0900, Sat from 1030, Sun from 0930

Reservations unnecessary

💳💳

International

💳💳

One of the most popular spots in this area, right on the main square, with acres of seating outside where people pose at the weekend, and a no-frills brasserie inside, serving steaks, salads and a few vegetarian dishes.

Le Garage ❺

Ruysdaelstraat 54–6

✆ 679 7176

🚊 Trams 3, 5 and 12

Open: daily for dinner and Mon–Fri lunch

Reservations essential

All credit cards accepted

French

💳💳💳

As chic as they come, this is one of the hippest places in Amsterdam, so make sure you dress the part. Thankfully the food is absolutely fabulous too, with brasserie fare boasting world influences, such as a cubed tuna tartare with curry.

De Knijp ❻

Van Baerlestraat 134

✆ 671 4248

🚊 Trams 3, 5, 12, 16, 20 and 24

Open: daily dinner and Mon–Fri lunch

Reservations recommended

All credit cards accepted

International

💳💳

There's split-level dining but an intimate atmosphere in this highly

▲ Beddington's

praised restaurant, which attracts visitors after they've been to the **Concertgebouw**. Dutch dishes such as goose breast sit alongside French and Italian offerings, like carpaccio with pesto.

De Orient

Van Baerlestraat 21
✆ 673 4958
🚊 Trams 2, 3, 5, 12 and 20
Open: daily from 1700
Reservations recommended
All credit cards accepted
Indonesian
❶❶

All Indonesian restaurants offer a *rijsttafel* but here it is a speciality with three meat and three vegetarian options available, depending on whether you think you can eat 12, 19 or 25 dishes between you.

Ristorante Mirafiori

Hobbemastraat 2
✆ 662 3013
🚊 Trams 2, 5 and 20
Open: Wed–Mon lunch and dinner
Reservations recommended
All credit cards accepted
Italian
❶❶

This smart Italian place is often rated as one of the city's best, and is much frequented by visiting celebrities. The dishes sound fairly ordinary – such as chicken in tomato sauce – but the cooking and intimate atmosphere make for a good evening.

Sama Sebo

Pieter Cornelisz Hoofdstraat 27
✆ 662 8146
🚊 Trams 2, 3, 5, 12 and 20
Open: Mon–Sat lunch and dinner
Reservations recommended
All credit cards accepted
Indonesian
❶❶

In this classy shopping street is this smart Indonesian restaurant with rush matting on the floor. Their special 20-dish *rijsttafel* is highly recommended and is regarded as one of the best such meals in town.

Trattoria Toto ❿

Eerste Constantijn Huygenstraat 112
✆ 683 0028
🚊 Trams 1, 3, 6 and 12
Open: daily for dinner
Reservations unnecessary
All credit cards accepted
Italian
❶❶

A very simple Italian trattoria of the type that you will find in almost any city in the world, except with others the cooking isn't always as good and fresh as this, from the garlic bread through to the pasta dishes and the terrific tiramisu.

▲ Café-Restaurant Wildshut

THE MUSEUM QUARTER
Bars, cafés and pubs

Brasserie Van Gogh 🄑

Pieter Cornelisz Hoofstraat 28

∅ No telephone

🚊 Trams 2, 3, 5, 12 and 20

Open: daily from 1000

€€

This bright corner café appeals unashamedly to the tourist visitors to the nearby **Van Gogh Museum** and **Rijksmuseum**. That said, and allowing for slightly high prices, it's a good place to take a break with pavement seating as well as a large interior. A wide range of drinks and snacks is available, including breakfasts, sandwiches, soups and light meals.

Café Ebeling 🄒

Overtoom 52

∅ 689 1218

🚊 Trams 1, 3, 6 and 12

Open: Mon–Sat from 1100, Sun from 1200

€

An enjoyable mix of a place with a split-level bar housed in what was a bank, where the toilets are in the old vaults.

The spacious public rooms attract a cross-section of young trendies, off-beat characters, arty people and an older and more dressed-down crowd.

Café Vertigo 🄓

Vondelpark

∅ 616 0611

🚊 Trams 1, 3, 6 and 12

Open: daily from 1100

€€

In a great location attached to the **Film Museum**, this café has a big terrace overlooking the park and a more intimate interior for dining at night by candlelight, as well as another indoor bar-restaurant area. The menu can change according to the film season showing, so you could have French, Italian, Dutch or Hollywood blockbusters on the menu.

Café Welling 🄔

Jan Willem Brouwerstraat 32

∅ 662 0155

🚊 Trams 2, 3, 5, 12, 16 and 20

Open: daily from 1500

€

An informal place close by the **Concertgebouw** which can therefore get rather busy – and certainly buzzy – before

▲ Café Vertigo

and after shows. It is popular with the audience and performers alike for its excellent choice of beers.

Dora's Blikkenbar 🔢

Vondelpark

∅ No telephone

🚊 Trams 1, 3, 6 and 12

Open: in summer during theatre performances

€

Not a proper bar but an Amsterdam tradition,

Dora sets up her little bar for performances at the **Vondelpark Openluchttheater** (Open Air Theatre) from June through to August. The bar sells beer and soft drinks in cans (*blikken* in Dutch) as well as crisps, sweets and other snacks.

Museum Eating

If you are planning a series of museum visits,

it is worth knowing that all three of the major museums in this area have somewhere to eat. Both the **Rijksmuseum** 🔢 and the **Van Gogh Museum** 🔢 have cafés, which also serve a good choice of hot dishes at lunchtime, while the **Stedelijk Museum** 🔢 has both a casual café and a more formal restaurant.

THE MUSEUM QUARTER
Shops, markets and picnic sites

Shops

Brandmeester's Coffee 19

Van Baerlestraat 13

✆ 675 7888

🚊 Trams 3, 12, 20 and 24

Open: Tue–Sat from 0900, Mon from 1200 and first Sun of month from 1200

Amsterdam may not have a surfeit of great food shops like other European cities, but it certainly has several excellent coffee- and teashops. This one concentrates on coffee and imports its own beans from all over the world and then roasts them on the premises. Resist the smell if you can.

Hendrikse Le Confiseur 20

Overtoom 448–50

✆ 618 0260

🚊 Trams 1 and 6

Open: Mon–Fri from 0845, Sat from 0830

One of Amsterdam's best and most inventive chocolate-makers, Hendrikse produces not just a wonderful range of handmade truffles and other conventional chocolates, but also sculpted figures of people and animals. He will even do one to order, if you want your favourite relative caricatured in chocolate.

Huize van Wely 21

Beethovenstraat 72

✆ 662 2009

🚊 Tram 5

▲ Huize van Wely

A chocolate shop not to be missed – the light and airy premises are filled with rows of tempting truffles in dozens of flavours, many of them alcoholic. There are also sumptuous cakes with a range of coloured icings, such as strawberry and lemon. Forget the diet and make up a selection.

De Pepperwortel 22

Overtoom 140

✆ 685 1053

🚊 Trams 1 and 6

Open: Mon–Fri from 1200, Sat–Sun from 1600

Handy for preparing picnics for the Vondelpark, this deli and general food store stocks a good selection of sandwiches and salads, or you could even buy one of their ready-made picnic hampers, depending on the number of people.

Renzo 23

Van Baerlestraat 67

✆ 673 1673

🚊 Trams 2, 3, 5, 12 and 20

Open: Mon–Sat from 0900, Sun from 1100

This great little deli has a range of breads, salads and cakes, all to take away or to eat on the premises at the long tables on the pavement outside. The atmosphere is slightly chaotic, but the prepared salads, pastas and other dishes are excellent.

▲ De Waterwinkel

De Waterwinkel 24

Roelof Hartstraat 10

✆ 675 5932

🚊 Trams 3, 5, 12 and 24

Open: Mon–Sat from 0900

A clean and cool-looking shop which specialises in selling water. Bottled waters from all around the world, more than 100 of them, line the shelves in sparkling rows.

Picnic sites

Vondelpark 25

🚊 Trams 1, 2, 3, 5, 6, 7, 10 and 12

Open: daily dawn till dusk

The largest green space in Amsterdam is naturally a favourite with the people of the city, who use it in many ways: to walk, to jog, to picnic, to take their children to play, to play with footballs and frisbees, and a few unofficial activities besides. It does make a great picnic spot, with numerous benches and pleasant places to relax around the ponds and lakes. There are one or two cafés as well as the **Café Vertigo** (*see page 52*) which overlooks the park. There aren't too many shops in the immediate vicinity to provide you with your picnic needs, so buy them on your way there.

Dutch gin

A knock on the head

The Dutch equivalent of gin is called *jenever*, although it is also made under this name in Belgium and elsewhere. It is not unlike the gin made in Britain and America, but it is slightly weaker and tastes a little bit thicker, not quite as clean tasting as gin itself. It is brewed from molasses and flavoured with juniper berries, although there are many types and flavours of *jenever* produced. Ask for a *jenever*, though, and you will be given the standard juniper *jenever*. The drink is also sometimes referred to as *Hollands*. You can also just ask for a glass, a *borrel*, or a small glass, known as a *borreltje*.

It is generally served in small glasses and drunk neat, and the Amsterdam tradition is to knock it back in one go, just as the Russians drink vodka. If you do this as a tourist trying the drink for the first time, it will undoubtedly be appreciated. It can be drunk at any time of the day or night, but is most commonly drunk, like gin, as an aperitif, but is also drunk with a glass of beer just as you might also drink a whisky chaser. If you want to try this combination, ask for a *kopstoot*. The literal meaning of this is a 'knock on the head', so you have been warned.

As with most spirits, it is the older and more matured *jenever* that is considered the best and is also the most expensive. *Oud* is the old type, which is generally very smooth indeed, making you realise that *jenever* is rather more complex a brew than straight gin. *Jong jenever* is obviously the young version, and this is rougher than the *oud* but it won't affect you as much as knocking back a glass of neat gin. It also won't affect your wallet as much, so if you take a liking to *jenever* do consider taking a bottle or two home, as if you buy it in the supermarkets it is a fraction of the cost of gin. If you want to take home a really good variety, though, or a particular flavour you may have been offered in a bar or restaurant, you will need to go to one of the specialist drinks shops such as **H P de Vreng en Zonen** (*see page 25*), who will have several dozen varieties.

The young version is also often mixed with something, such as coke or tonic water, to take away the roughness – a sacrilege you would never do with the mature *jenever*. If you're served a neat glass which is full to the brim then you're being challenged to drink it in the traditional way, which is to lean over and take the glass between your lips and drink it 'hands-off' without spilling a drop! A glass served in this way is known as a *kamelenrug*, which it is not surprising to learn means 'a camel's back', after the meniscus shape.

There are all kinds of flavours and mixes available, and you might want to try *bitterje*, which is *jenever* with angostura bitters, or something like *bessenjenever*, which is *jenever* flavoured with blackcurrants. See the Menu decoder (*pages 90–3*) under the section for Fruits for the many other flavours with which *jenever* might be imbued, such as lemon.

> **The Amsterdam tradition is to knock it back in one go, just as the Russians drink vodka.**

To sample a good range of *jenevers* you need to visit a *proeflokaal* or tasting house, though not all of these serve *jenever*, as some may be tasting houses for breweries rather than distilleries, like the **Brouwerij 't Ij** (*see page 82*). One of the most famous *jenever* palaces in Amsterdam is **De Drie Fleschjes** (*see page 12*) which dates back to 1650. Like many such places, its opening hours are quite short, reflecting the fact that *jenever* is mainly an aperitif. During the week it will be closed by 2030, and by 1900 on Sundays, but in the hours that it is open it does a roaring trade especially from local workers calling in for a quick one before going home. Many regulars have their own barrels, which they slowly work their way through over the years.

Another good *proeflokaal* for *jenever* is **De Admiraal** (*see page 22*). This is more like a regular bar than the traditional De Drie Fleschjes, and stays open till the early hours, serving up not just 15 different kinds of *jenever* but a few dozen types of liqueur too, as well as regular beers and wines, plus hot meals and snacks to boot.

De Pijp

This multi-cultural area to the south of the centre is one of the most diverse in Amsterdam, and has not yet been discovered by too many visitors. That's a shame as it's lively and friendly, with a range of good inexpensive restaurants, cafés and bars, and with easily the city's best market along Albert Cuypstraat.

DE PIJP
Restaurants

Cambodja City ❶

Albert Cuypstraat 58–60	
✆ 671 4930	
🚊 Trams 16, 24 and 25	
Open: Tue–Sat from 1100, Sun from 1400	
Reservations unnecessary	
No credit cards accepted	
Asian	
❻	

This ordinary-looking restaurant serves excellent inexpensive spicy food from Vietnam, Thailand and Cambodia, with dishes such as Vietnam ginger chicken and Thai chicken curry on offer. Ignore the surroundings and enjoy the taste sensations.

Le Ciel Bleu ❷

23rd Floor, Okura Hotel, Ferdinand Bolstraat 333	
✆ 678 7111	
🚊 Trams 12 and 25	
Open: daily for dinner and Sun brunch from 1130	
Reservations essential	
All credit cards accepted	
French	
❻❻❻	

'The Blue Sky' is aptly named given how close it is to the heavens, and the elegant interior has a star-filled night-sky painted ceiling. Gourmet French cuisine and matching wine list and, unusually, two set vegetarian menus.

De Duvel ❸

1e Van der Helstraat 59–61	
✆ 675 7517	
🚊 Trams 16, 24 and 25	
Open: daily from about 1200	
Reservations unnecessary	
All credit cards accepted	

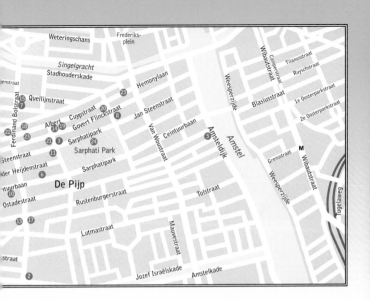

▲ Smoked fish salad

▲ Siempre

International
⊘⊘

Popular café-bar-restaurant with some outdoor seating near the **Albert Cuypmarkt** (*see page 65*). Lunchtime dishes are simple such as steak sandwiches and tuna salads, but in the evening there are more adventurous alternatives.

Le Hollandais ❺

Amsteldijk 41

café siempre tapas

⊘ 679 1248

🚊 Tram 4

Open: daily for dinner

Reservations essential

💳 💳

French-International
⊘⊘

A very fashionable restaurant by the Amstel whose chef serves up unusual regional food with Dutch, French and other influences. There is also always a fish of the day, and anchovies with tuna, olives and mint is one starter.

The India Cottage ❻

Ceintuurbaan 111

⊘ 662 8873

🚊 Trams 3, 12, 16, 20, 24 and 25

Open: daily for dinner

Reservations unnecessary

All credit cards accepted

Indian
⊘

An excellent Indian place with pleasing authentic decoration and friendly waiters. They specialise in balti dishes, but also biriyani and dansak dishes, along with a whole host of other Indian and Pakistani options.

Ondeugd ❼

Ferdinand Bolstraat 15

⊘ 672 0651

🚊 Trams 3, 6, 7, 10, 12, 16, 20, 24 and 25

Open: Mon–Sat dinner only

Reservations recommended

All credit cards accepted

French

Ondeugd is incredibly popular and attracts media people, soccer stars and other celebs. The menu might need translating for you – would you know 'TV Chef' was fish with chutney? Grilled tuna fillet in a Japanese dressing is more obvious.

Siempre **8**

1e Sweelinckstraat 23
7 671 8616
Trams 3, 4 and 20
Open: daily from 1600
Reservations recommended
No credit cards accepted
Spanish

Characterful Spanish *tapas* bar-restaurant with hams hanging from the ceiling and dishes such as tortilla with *chorizo* and shrimp croquettes on the menu, along with *raciones* (larger portions).

Trez **9**

Saenredamstraat 39–41
7 676 2495
Trams 6, 7, 10, 16, 24 and 25
Open: daily for dinner
Reservations recommended
No credit cards accepted
French

This is a lovely place which you might not be able to see behind all the greenery outside. Fricassee of rabbit in beer and mustard is one example of the interesting food on offer from the open kitchen in the middle of the restaurant.

Witteveen **10**

Ceintuurbaan 256
7 662 4368
Trams 3, 12, 20, 24 and 25
Open: daily for dinner
Reservations recommended

All credit cards accepted

Dutch

This is probably the best place in De Pijp to sample Dutch cooking that doesn't ignore outside influences, as the entrecôte with truffle butter and the sautéed salmon with lemongrass indicate. Good, intimate Amsterdam atmosphere.

▲ Siempre

DE PIJP
Bars, cafés and pubs

Café Krull ⑪

Sarphatipark 2

✆ 662 0214

🚊 Trams 3, 4, 16 and 20

Open: daily from 1100

€

A very attractive café-bar with a light and airy feel, thanks to the large windows, and a relaxed atmosphere with newspapers around and a noticeboard for local and artistic events. A place where people seem happy to relax with a beer or coffee, alone or with friends, and bar snacks are available all day long.

Carel's Café ⑫

Frans Halsstraat 76

✆ 679 4836

🚊 Trams 16, 24 and 25

Open: Mon–Sat from 1000, Sun from 1100

€

The perfect neighbourhood café-bar, on a quiet corner with outdoor seating where everyone can relax; the old, the young and family parties. The food is especially good, with some hot meals but mainly snacks, though the rolls use delicious bread and are packed with flavour: try the mozzarella, tomato and basil, and see what you think.

Gambrinus ⑬

Ferdinand Bolstraat 180

✆ 671 7389

🚊 Trams 16, 24 and 25

Open: daily from 1100

€

A bright and friendly corner café-bar on one of De Pijp's main streets. The bustle adds to the busy feel of the place, especially when the **Albert Cuypmarkt** (*see page 65*) is in full

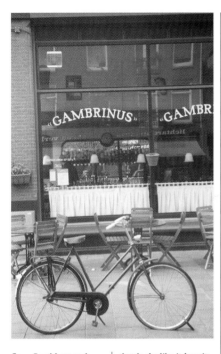

Open: daily from 1100

Right behind the Heineken Brewery is this Irish pub that follows the formula for Irish pubs worldwide, though it's a bit less rowdy than those in the city centre, thanks to its location on the edge of De Pijp. It still offers live sport on large-screen TVs in the back bar, and live music in the front bar, and it's a huge place but often full.

't Ezeltje

Cornelis Troostsstraat 56–8

✆ 662 1703

🚊 Trams 12 and 25

Open: daily from 1600

A very ordinary-looking bar from the outside, but this popular place is one of the best and liveliest brown cafés in the area with a wider than average selection of beers and simple but good-quality bar snacks. Leave it too late and you'll struggle to get in.

flow. Good beer and tasty food is what makes it popular, plus the Sunday live music sessions.

Granny

1e Van der Helstraat 45

✆ 679 4465

🚊 Trams 3, 4, 16 and 20

Open: daily

A busy little café near the Albert Cuypmarkt which appeals more to families and shoppers looking for a coffee and a cake. It serves a big range of snacks and sandwiches in a room

that looks like it hasn't changed in fifty years.

O'Donnell's

Ferdinand Bolstraat 5

✆ 676 7786

🚊 Trams 16, 24 and 25

DE PIJP
Shops, markets and picnic sites

Book 'n' Serve ⓱

Ferdinand Bolstraat 151–3

∅ 664 3446

Ⓣ Trams 3, 12, 20, 24 and 25

Open: Mon from 1200, Tue–Sat from 0930

Not many internet cafés merit a mention as cafés in their own right, but this bright and pleasant place does. Pass through the bookshop and up the stairs to a small seating area, where you can have fresh coffees or fresh orange juice, and on Saturday mornings hot croissants too, and beyond the café there are the internet facilities.

Casa Molero ⓲

Gerard Doustraat 66

∅ 676 1707

Ⓣ Trams 16, 24 and 25

Open: Tue–Sat from 0900

Walk one block north of Albert Cuypstraat to find this Iberian delicatessen and general food store, another contribution to the ethnic mix of the area, and supplier to local bars and cafés of their *tapas* basics. It sells a wonderful array of hams and sausages from Spain, along with cheeses, breads, herbs, spices and other cooking ingredients. There is also an off-licence section where both Spanish and Portuguese wines are stocked.

De Cuyp ⓳

Albert Cuypstraat 146

∅ 662 6676

Ⓣ Trams 3, 4, 12, 16, 20, 24 and 25

Open: Tue–Sat from 0900

A huge sign in the **Albert Cuypmarkt** (*see below*) directs you to this large liquor store, and although it initially looks like just another outlet for cheap gin and whisky, inside is a bigger stock than you might expect. In addition to the big brand names for spirits, where there are bargains to be had, there are also top-quality wines at good prices, dozens of bottled beers, including many excellent Belgian brands, some 3 000 miniatures for people who collect those, and spirits and liqueurs from all over the world, catering to the ethnic mix of the neighbourhood.

Sareleng Atin ⓴

1e Sweelinckstraat 20

∅ 673 4309

Ⓣ Trams 3, 4, 16, 20, 24 and 25

Open: Mon–Sat from 1000

An indication of the variety of inhabitants in De Pijp is the existence of this Filipino food and drink store just off the Albert Cuypmarkt. Loose and packaged spices, pre-packed food, dried food and fresh food are all available. You may not want to buy, unless you've a particular interest in the cookery of the country, but it is certainly worth a look for those that are curious.

Tjin's Toko ㉑

1e Van der Helstraat 64

∅ 671 7708

▲ Albert Cuypmarkt

▲ Sarphati Park

◉ Trams 3, 4, 12, 16, 20, 24 and 25

Open: Mon–Sat from 0900

Two blocks away from the Albert Cuypmarkt is this little store which stocks a mix of Asian and American foodstuffs and drinks, as well as cooking spices and utensils. A small delicatessen counter sells unusual salads and snacks too.

Toko Ramee ㉒

Ferdinand Bolstraat 74

✆ 662 2025

◉ Trams 16, 20, 24 and 25

Open: Tue–Sat from 0900

Facing the top of the Albert Cuypmarkt is this specialist store which sells lots of general household goods from Asia, but also has a large number of spices and other cooking ingredients for sale, particularly from Indonesia, China and Thailand, as well as takeaway snacks.

Markets

Albert Cuypmarkt ㉓

Albert Cuypstraat

◉ Trams 3, 4, 12, 16, 20, 24 and 25

Open: Mon–Sat

The city's biggest and best street market, which has general household goods and clothes, but plenty of food stalls too. De Pijp is a multi-cultural area and this is reflected in the produce on display, with many exotic fruit and vegetables from Asia, Africa and the Caribbean. Dutch produce can be seen on several cheese stalls, some with pieces of Edam and Gouda the size of car tyres, along with delicacies such as olives, pre-prepared salads, sausages and other tempting food that makes you want to have

a picnic even if you hadn't planned one – and the **Sarphati Park** (*see below*) is only two streets away.

Picnic sites

Sarphati Park ㉔

◉ Trams 3, 4, 12, 16, 20, 24 and 25

Open: daily, dawn till dusk

A perfect little park to retreat to and sit in after putting together a picnic from the Albert Cuypmarkt and the various delicatessens, bakeries, patisseries and other food shops in the area. There are several ponds and pathways, places to sit, fountains and a children's play area. It is only small but it proves to be a popular family park for the people in the neighbourhood.

The Heineken story

A worldwide phenomenon

Drink and help to save the world. Well, it's true if you visit the Heineken Brewery which overlooks the Singelgracht canal, not far from the **Rijksmuseum**. The small admission fee you pay to join a tour of the brewery, which includes free drinks, is donated to worthy charities such as the World Wide Fund for Nature.

Heineken is arguably the best-known beer in the world, dominating markets as Coca Cola does for soft drinks, so that in some countries if you ask for a beer you will automatically be served a Heineken. Even in countries where you may be given a choice, it is often

between Amstel and Heineken, both Dutch brews, which proves that this small nation has given the world more than just Van Gogh and Rembrandt.

The brewery on this site dates back to 1592, and was known as **De Hooiberg Brewery** ('The Haystack') until it was bought in 1863 by a 22-year-old Dutchman named Gerard Adriaan Heineken. That was the start of the Heineken dynasty at this site, though Adriaan Heineken had already made a name for himself as a brewer. It was a name that was to spread throughout the world.

The Heineken Brewery is no longer a working brewery, as it was forced to close in 1988 due to the problems of distributing their constantly increasing production when locked in the middle of Amsterdam, with its canals and small streets. You don't have to spend long in Amsterdam to see the problems that larger delivery lorries have in negotiating the narrow one-way streets, especially alongside the canals.

The Heineken Brewery was kept open as a visitor centre, though, and by joining one of the set tours you can hear the Heineken story and see how the brew was made, as some of the plant has been kept intact. You can see the fermentation tanks, each having the capacity to hold a million glasses of Heineken. A short video film is projected on multi-screens to tell you the history of brewing and of Heineken, through to the closing down of this brewery.

But don't worry, as although they no longer make Heineken here, the brew is naturally available at the end of the tour. In theory there are two complimentary glasses per person, plus some snacks, which is not a bad deal in itself for your small admission fee. In practice you can have another glass or two if you wish, as the atmosphere is very cordial, as you can imagine when the tours are usually full, meaning there are 150 people in the centre enjoying the company's generous hospitality. Heineken has the good sense to know that if the company is using this tour to boost their image, it would undermine the whole point if they were seen to be stingy at the end. In fact if you can prove that it's your birthday, you'll be given an impressive Delftware Heineken beer mug.

From a financial point of view the company has no need to stint on offering its fans and would-be fans a few free drinks. You will learn statistics such as the fact that it is sold in about 170 countries around the world, and is the number one imported beer in the United States. In Amsterdam alone people drink an astonishing 80,000 bottles of Heineken *per hour.* You are not bombarded with

statistics, though, and there is a short tasting stop about halfway through the hour-long tour. You also get to see the shire horses that are still used to haul drays around the city streets, but purely for promotional purposes and for the sake of keeping up the tradition, rather than because it is still a viable delivery method. Well, at the rate the Amsterdammers drink it, the brew would have to be delivered by racehorses to keep up with the demand.

In Amsterdam alone people drink an astonishing 80,000 bottles of Heineken per hour.

• **Heineken Brewery (Heineken Brouwerij)** *78 Stadhouderskade; ℂ 523 9666;* trams *6, 7, 10, 16, 20, 24 and 25; open: Mon–Fri at 0930 and 1100; from 1 June–5 Sept extra tours at 1300 and 1430; on Sat in Aug also at 1100, 1300 and 1430.*
Participants may not be younger than 18. Tours cannot be booked in advance and, since the maximum number of participants per tour is 150 and is subject to availability, you should arrive in good time. The nominal admission fee is donated in its entirety to institutions such as the Red Cross, the World Wide Fund for Nature and other charities.

Rembrandtplein

The Rembrandtplein is where various faces of Amsterdam meet – the culture of Rembrandt whose house is nearby, the history of the Jewish quarter, the trade of the flower market and the sleaze of a smaller red light district with a handful of strip clubs. Eating options are also mixed, with grand cafés, exotic cuisines and traditional Dutch restaurants alike.

REMBRANDTPLEIN
Restaurants

Brasserie Schiller ❶

Hotel Schiller,
Rembrandtplein 26–36

✆ 554 0700

🚋 Trams 4, 9, 14 and 20

Open: daily from 0700

Reservations recommended

All credit cards accepted

French-International

€€

Another of Amsterdam's grand dining spaces, the vaulted ceiling of the century-old Schiller looks down on diners enjoying classic French dishes such as Filet Véronique and other traditional European meals too, like roast leg of lamb with mint sauce.

Kort ❷

Amstelveld 12

✆ 626 1199

🚋 Tram 4

Open: Wed–Mon from 1130

Reservations recommended

All credit cards accepted

International

€€

Housed in a wooden 17th-century former church alongside a canal (reserve a terrace table if you can), the food here matches the view. Eastern spiced fish is a house special, or try Moroccan fish *tajine*.

Maison Descartes ❸

Vijzelgracht 2A

✆ 622 1913

🚋 Trams 6, 7, 10, 16, 20, 24 and 25

Open: Mon–Fri lunch and dinner

Reservations essential

No credit cards accepted

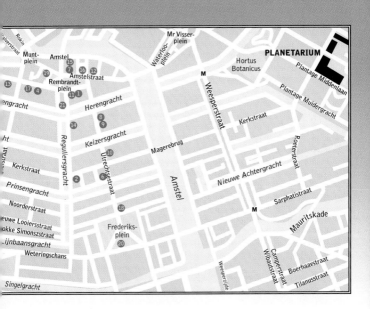

French

❷❸

This elegant little restaurant is in the same building as the French Consulate, whose staff regularly dine here, indicating the high French standards it sets. The fact that you would need to book several weeks ahead is another testament to its culinary reputation.

Memories of India ❹

Reguliersdwarsstraat 88

∅ 623 5710

🚊 Trams 4, 9, 14 and 20

Open: daily for dinner

Reservations unnecessary

All credit cards accepted

Indian

❷❸

One of the city's most sophisticated Indian restaurants with impeccable service and palatial décor. Even side dishes such as poppadoms and naans are prepared with care, and the lamb vindaloo is one of their special dishes.

Le Pêcheur ❺

Reguliersdwarsstraat 32

∅ 624 3121

🚊 Trams 1, 2 and 5

Open: Mon–Fri from 1200, Sat from 1700

Reservations recommended

💳 🔲 American Express

Seafood

❷❸

If you are dining in the summer ask for a garden table and enjoy the flowers (it's very near the flower market), along with the sophisticated fish dishes such as fried wolf-fish with a light mustard sauce.

Les Quatre Canetons ❻

Prinsengracht 1111

∅ 624 6307

🚊 Tram 4

Open: Mon–Fri lunch and dinner, Sat dinner

Reservations essential

All credit cards accepted

International

❷❸❹

A rural retreat restaurant right in the city,

▲ Brasserie Schiller

with a delightful hidden garden behind a 17th-century canal house. It's justifiably popular for dishes such as roasted whole lobster with lobster risotto and small vegetables in a foamy lobster gravy.

Royal Café de Kroon ❼

Rembrandtplein 17

✆ 625 2011

🚊 Trams 4, 9, 14 and 20

Open: daily from 1000

Reservations unnecessary

💳 🏧 American Express

International

💰💰

In this huge, airy space with high ceilings in Grand Café style and a palm court orchestra on Sunday, eating here is always an experience. Food consists of simple staples such as salmon or steaks, but de Kroon remains a local favourite.

Sluizer ❽

Utrechtsestraat 43

✆ 622 6376

🚊 Tram 4

Open: daily for dinner, and Mon–Fri lunch

Reservations recommended

All credit cards accepted

International

💰💰

The Sluizer has been so successful it recently split in two (*see below*) with this location known as the 'Specialities Restaurant' with a dark wood-panelled décor. Meat-eaters

This branch of the Sluizer with its marble-topped tables focuses on its highly-rated fish dishes, of which fish stew (*waterzooi*) has become an established menu favourite. Scallops, octopus or the day's fresh catch are other options.

Tempo Doeloe

Utrechtsestraat 75

☎ 625 6718

🚊 Tram 4

Open: daily for dinner

Reservations unnecessary

All credit cards accepted

Indonesian

💶💶

Batik, candles and Indonesian puppets set the tone for this relaxing place which has a superior Indonesian menu to most. Try goat cooked in coconut milk, cardamom and sweet spices, or giant prawn with coconut and curry.

can tuck into dishes such as beef stroganoff, though there are vegetarian options too.

Sluizer Visrestaurant

Utrechtsestraat 45

☎ 626 3557

🚊 Tram 4

Open: daily for dinner and Mon–Fri lunch

Reservations recommended

All credit cards accepted

Seafood

💶💶

▲ Les Quatre Cantons

REMBRANDTPLEIN
Bars, cafés and pubs

Café Schiller

Rembrandtplein 26

✆ 624 9846

🚊 Trams 4, 9, 14 and 20

Open: daily from 1600, hot meals from 1730

What was formerly the bar at the four-star **Schiller Hotel** is a smarter option than many in the Rembrandtplein area, parts of which can be rather seedy – but the Schiller is an art-deco retreat where you'll pay a little more but can sip your drinks in what is now a fashionable media watering hole.

Cooldown

Rembrandtplein 45

✆ 638 9242

🚊 Trams 4, 9, 14 and 20

Open: daily from 2000

Be sure that this is your kind of bar before venturing in, although the photos around the doors of customers enjoying themselves in various stages of undress and various stages of inebriation will give you some idea of the brash party place that it is. Perfect if that's what you're into.

L'Entrée

Reguliersdwarsstraat 42

✆ 623 0543

🚊 Trams 4, 9, 14, 16, 20, 24 and 25

Open: daily from 2100

This late-night drinking bar offers a refuge to the slightly more sophisticated crowd in this often rowdy and heavy-drinking area. High ceilings, a long bar and plush seats help keep the atmosphere relaxed in what was once a rather grand 19th-century town-house.

Hooghoudt Bar

Reguliersgracht 11

✆ 420 4041

🚊 Trams 4, 9, 14 and 20

Open: Tue–Fri from 1600, Sat–Sun from 1200

A bar that's the public face of the Hooghoudt distillery, which produces a range of strong *jenevers* (gins), so there ought to be nowhere better to try them than here, though perhaps not all on the same night. There is also a restaurant beyond the bar, if you want a simple meal as well.

Mulligans

Amstel 100

✆ 622 1330

🚊 Trams 4, 9, 14, 16, 20, 24 and 25

Open: Mon–Fri from 1600, Sat–Sun from 1400

This Irish pub on the banks of the Amstel is better than most, with a chatty atmosphere that's more to do with people having a good time talking, drinking and listening to music, rather than going in simply to get drunk, as happens in many of the bars nearer to the city centre.

L'Opéra

Rembrandtplein 27–9

✆ 627 5232

🚊 Trams 4, 9, 14, 20

Open: daily from 1000, hot meals from 1100

A place decked out in Grand Café style that's right on the Rembrandtplein and has outdoor seating to watch the passing parade – and in Amsterdam there always is one – and indoors a Parisian atmosphere of mirrored reds and golds.

't Madeliefje

Reguliersdwarsstraat 76

✆ 622 2510

🚊 Trams 4, 9, 14, 16, 20, 24 and 25

Open: Tue–Sat from 2100
❻

The Dutch love salsa and like to show off their skills here on a Wednesday night, though there's music every night and the bar is popular with a smart set in their 20s and 30s, making it a much pleasanter place than many bars hereabouts.

▲ L'Opéra

REMBRANDTPLEIN
Shops, markets and picnic sites

Shops

Elzinga Wijnen ⑱
Fredericksplein 1
☎ 623 7270

🚊 Tram 4
Open: Mon–Tue from 1300,
Wed–Sat from 1000

Only a small shop but one of the best of a limited range of wine shops in Amsterdam, this stocks quality wines mainly from France, Italy, Spain and Portugal – new world wines are still too expensive for the

▲ Kwekkeboom

▲ Frederiksplein

quality available, compared to European types.

Kwekkeboom ⑲

Reguliersbreestraat 36

✆ 623 1205

🚊 Trams 4, 9, 14 and 20

Open: Mon–Sat from 0900

There are a few branches of the Kwekkeboom patisserie, but this is one of the bigger ones. The small chain of stores has won numerous accolades for its cakes, pastries and especially its chocolates, which use the best quality ingredients, and you should certainly try a selection: prices are high but you get what you pay for.

> **Picnic sites**

Frederiksplein ⑳

🚊 Trams 4, 6, 7, 10 and 20

There is a dearth of good picnic spots in this busy area, but the little open area around Frederiksplein is pleasant enough, with a fountain and some seating in among the small areas of trees and bushes.

Thorbekeplein ㉑

🚊 Trams 4, 9, 14 and 20

Not the typical kind of airy open space where you can picnic, but quite a wide street in the middle of which is an arts and crafts market, and along the edges are benches which do make good spectator spots if you want to have a cheap lunch munching on a sandwich.

Indonesian food

A touch of the exotic

What do we mean by traditional food? There are some dishes described on menus as being traditionally Dutch and yet they will have been around for nowhere nearly as long as Indonesian food has in the Dutch capital. The most famous Indonesian dish of all, the *rijsttafel* (rice table), was brought to Amsterdam as long ago as the 17th century by traders in the Dutch East India Company. It was popular here even before the first Indonesian immigrants arrived and perpetuated the dish when they opened restaurants to cater for both their own people and the Dutch liking for exotic Indonesian cuisine.

The *rijsttafel* is like a Greek or Middle Eastern *meze*, a range of small dishes which gives the customer an indication of the variety available and allows the

> ... a range of tastes and textures, sweet-and-sour combinations, soft and crunchy textures, contrasting mild and hot sauces ...

restaurant to show off its skills with different combinations. A *rijsttafel* can usually only be ordered by two people, although some restaurants will serve it for one while others offer different sizes and prices, letting you know how many different plates each one contains. A typical *rijsttafel* will have anywhere from 15 to 25 dishes. Admittedly they are only small portions, but do not overlook the fact that you are ordering a very substantial meal. If there are several of you dining you may be able to opt for thirty dishes or even more. Be guided by the restaurateur.

Other cuisines in Amsterdam have copied the idea, so you may find a *rijsttafel* on the menu in Indian, Chinese, Japanese and other Asian restaurants. The base of the meal will be rice, and all the dishes will be brought at once, kept warm on the table on several heating devices. The idea is to present a range of tastes and textures, so there will be sweet-and-sour combinations, soft and crunchy textures, contrasting mild and hot sauces (and beware the hot ones which can be quite a shock to the unwary palate). Unless you are an expert, simply dip in and experiment, or if the

INDONESIAN FOOD

▲ *Rijsttafel* spread at Puri Mas

restaurant is not too busy the waiters may have time to talk you through the dishes and suggest ways of tackling them. Don't forget that the idea is to sample a little from all of the dishes, and not take just a few whole dishes for yourself.

One dish that is sure to appear in most *rijsttafels* and separately on Indonesian menus is *gado gado*. This is a mixture of whatever vegetables are seasonal, with a mild and creamy peanut sauce stirred in. Peanut sauce features a lot in Indonesian dishes, perhaps the best known being pork *saté*, these being small cubes of pork which are grilled kebab-style and served with a slightly spicy peanut sauce.

MENU DECODER

ajam – chicken
babi ketjap – pork in soy sauce
bami – noodles with meat and vegetables
bami goreng – fried noodles with meat and vegetables
daging – beef
daging smoor – beef in soy sauce
gado gado – vegetables in peanut sauce
goreng – fried
ikan – fish
katjang – peanut
kerriesoep – curry soup
kip met kerriesaus en rijst – chicken with curry sauce and rice
kroepoek – prawn crackers
loempia – spring rolls
nasi – rice
nasi goreng – fried rice with meat and vegetables
nasi rames – several dishes on one plate
pedis – very hot and spicy
perkedel – meatballs
pisang – banana
pisang goreng – fried banana
rijsttafel – selection of several different dishes, usually only served for two people, with plain rice
roedjak manis – fruit in a sweet sauce
sambal – very hot chilli sauce
saté – peanut sauce
seroendeng – fried coconut
tauge – bean sprouts
zoet-zuur – sweet-sour

The Plantage and the Oost

The east of the city centre is barely touched upon by most visitors, making it a place of exploration. The rewards are plenty of parks and markets, inexpensive restaurants with international cuisines such as Spanish, Portuguese, French and African, and a feeling that you're finding a part of the city you can regard as your own little discovery.

THE PLANTAGE AND THE OOST
Restaurants

B&W Café ❶

Plantage Kerklaan 36

∅ 422 8989

🚊 Trams 6, 9, 14 and 20

Open: daily from 1100

Reservations unnecessary

All credit cards accepted

International

❻

This casual media café has live music most nights and the food is good too, with weekly specials such as fried mussels, and a menu with two meat, two fish and one vegetarian option, plus Dutch specials.

Girassol ❷

Weesperzijde 135

∅ 692 3471

🚊 Trams 6, 7, 10 and 20 or to Amstelstation

Open: daily for dinner

Reservations recommended

All credit cards accepted

Portuguese

❻❻

Family-run and welcoming, this is a bit of a way out but serves some of the best Portuguese food in the city. Look out over the Amstel and enjoy grilled sardines or swordfish steaks, washed down with good Portuguese wine.

Iberia ❸

Hoogte Kadijksplein 16

∅ 623 6313

🚊 Trams 6 and 20

Open: daily for dinner

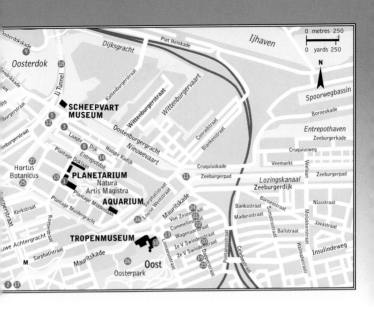

Reservations recommended

All credit cards accepted

Spanish-Portuguese

Hidden away in this quieter part of the city is this lively place that brings a touch of Iberia to Amsterdam, in both décor and cuisine. Try *escalope de vaca con porto*, *tapas* or the house speciality, a rich fish and seafood stew called *zarzuela*.

Jerusalem of Gold ❹

Jodenbreestraat 148

✆ 625 0923

🚋 Trams 9, 14 and 20

Open: daily, closed Jewish holidays

Reservations unnecessary

No credit cards accepted

Kosher

This unpretentious little café-restaurant is rec-

ommended by staff at the nearby **Jewish Historical Museum**. Despite the city's Jewish connections there are few Jewish eating places, and while the food here is simple, it is at least kosher.

Kilimanjaro ❺

Rapenburgerplein 6

✆ 622 3485

🚌 Bus 22 or take a tram to Centraal Station and walk

Open: Tue–Sun dinner

Reservations recommended

No credit cards accepted

African

❻

From Moroccan dishes cooked in the *tajine* to antelope from Tanzania, this East African specialist restaurant, with more of a café look to it, produces all kinds of exotic dishes cooked up by the Ethiopian chef.

De Magere Brug ❻

Amstel 81

✆ 622 6502

🚋 Trams 9, 14 and 20

Open: daily lunch and dinner

Reservations recommended

All credit cards accepted

Dutch

❻❻

Named after 'The Skinny Bridge' which it overlooks, this homely Dutch place with a relaxed feel and look is helping keep Dutch culinary traditions alive, especially with dishes such as smoked eel. Fresh fish is always available too.

La Rive ❼

Amstel Intercontinental Hotel, Professor Tulpplein 1

✆ 622 6060

🚋 Trams 6, 7, 10 and 20

Open: Mon–Fri lunch and dinner, Sat dinner

Reservations essential

All credit cards accepted

French

🟡🟡🟡

One of Amsterdam's landmark restaurants, with two Michelin stars and the atmosphere of an old-fashioned gentlemen's club. The food is anything but old-fashioned, with exquisite dishes such as guinea fowl with a cream of white beans, rosemary and sherry vinegar.

Saudade 8

Entrepotdok 36

∅ 625 4845

🟢 Trams 6 and 20

Open: daily for dinner

Reservations recommended

All credit cards accepted

Portuguese

🟡🟡

The Entrepotdok area is well known to the locals but has not really been discovered by many visitors yet. One of the best of the handful of eating places is Saudade, serving Portuguese food with an emphasis on fresh fish and *tapas*-style snacks.

Sea Palace 9

Oosterdokskade

∅ 626 4777

🟢 Any tram or bus to Centraal Station

Open: daily from 1200

Reservations unnecessary

All credit cards accepted

Chinese

🟡🟡

A vast floating restaurant (claimed to be the first in Europe), with a mock pagoda outside and three floors inside, seating 900 people. The mainly Cantonese menu is equally extensive, and though food on this scale is seldom outstanding, the dining experience is.

Soeterijn 10

Linnaeusstraat 2

∅ 568 8392

🟢 Trams 7, 9, 10 and 14

Open: Tue–Fri lunch, Mon–Sat dinner

Reservations recommended

All credit cards accepted

African-Asian

🟡🟡

Linked to the **Tropenmuseum** next door, which showcases the developing world, Soeterijn is an unusual café-type restaurant that highlights the cuisines of the mainly African and Asian countries featured in the museum.

THE PLANTAGE AND THE OOST
Bars, cafés and pubs

Brouwerij t'Ij 11

Funenkade 7

☎ 622 8325

🚊 Trams 7 and 10

Open: Wed–Sun from 1500

☕

The windmill makes this place unmissable, and the bar is a part of the small independent brewery named **Ij**. Brewery tours take place every Friday at 1600, and the bar is crowded most of the time it's open as it's popular with locals, as well as being on the map for beer-loving visitors. The Brouwerij t'Ij only sells its own beers, but there are about ten of them, all available on draught.

Café de Druif 12

Rapenburgerplein 83

☎ 624 4530

🚍 Bus 22 or trams 6 and 20

Open: daily from 1100

☕

A fantastic little bar just out of the city centre with a real neighbourhood feel to it. It's tiny inside with split-level seating and other seating around the sides of the main room, giving it an intimate and friendly atmosphere. It offers all the usual range of beers, wines and coffees, plus spirits and liqueurs arrayed in bottles and barrels behind the bar.

East of Eden 13

Linnaeusstraat 11a

☎ 665 0743

🚊 Trams 7, 9, 10 and 14

Open: daily from 1100

☕☕

This café-bar with a touch of the Orient about it – high ceilings, palm trees, cane furniture – serves quick and easy dishes such as *tapas*, guacamole, tomato soup, pâtés and cheeses. The owner cheerfully owns up that the *tapas* are bought in and microwaved, which is nothing unusual, though the honesty is, showing what a relaxed place it is in which to while away a few drinks.

Entredok 14

Entrepotdok 61

☎ 623 2356

🚊 Trams 6 and 20

Open: daily from lunchtime

☕

A great bar in this quiet but characterful

converted dock area which has a real sense of community. The bar is quite new but amazingly looks as old and as welcoming as any in Amsterdam, with magazines lying around for you to read. As well as drinks it serves good food too, such as tagliatelle with spinach and mushrooms and other *tapas* and pasta dishes.

Grand Café de Plantage ⓯

Plantage Middenlaan
✆ 421 6061
🚊 Trams 6, 9, 14 and 20
Open: daily from 1100
€

This brasserie-style place doesn't quite merit the 'Grand Café' tag but it's a pleasant option for a coffee or a simple snack (steaks, salads, sandwiches, plus daily specials), with seating on the pavement, a cosy bar and lots of seating inside too. It's just down the street from the **zoo**'s main entrance and is the kind of place that has children's meals on the menu as well.

De Groene Olifant ⓰

Sarphatistraat 510
✆ 620 4904
🚊 Trams 7, 9, 10 and 14
Open: daily from 1100
€

With a terrace right by the Old City Gate and a great range of Dutch and Belgian beers, both on tap and by the bottle, this friendly bar

▲ Hesp

('The Green Elephant') also serves basic snacks, including soups and salads.

Hesp ⓱

Weesperzijde 130
✆ 665 1202
🚊 Tram 12 or Amstelstation
Open: daily from 1000
€

This is quite a trek from the centre, but if you want a stroll along the Amstel on a sunny day then head in this direction, as it's an old and welcoming bar of great character, which locals know and love but few tourists see. There are seats outside as well, looking across the Amstel, and inside beyond the well-stocked bar another large seating area. Bar snacks are available too.

newMetropolis Café ⓲

Oosterdok 2
✆ 0900 919 1100
🚊 Bus 22, in summer shuttle bus from Centraal Station

Open: daily from 1000
€

This café enjoys one of the undoubtedly best settings in the city on the top of the **newMetropolis Science Museum**, which looks like a boat about to set sail into Amsterdam's harbours. It's the perfect place for a coffee and a snack while admiring the views of the city, but there are better places for your main meal of the day.

▲ newMetropolis Science Museum

THE PLANTAGE AND THE OOST
Shops, markets and picnic sites

▲ Dappermarkt

Shops

Boer Geert 19

Dapperstraat 82

🚋 Trams 3, 7, 10 and 14

Open: Mon–Sat

A European delicatessen which stocks various breads, and dozens of cheeses, hams and salamis.

Ghazi's 20

Dapperplein 9

🚋 Trams 3, 7, 10 and 14

Open: Mon–Sat

Set on the square halfway along Dapperstraat is Ghazi's, a Middle-Eastern food store-cum-supermarket filled to the gills with fruit, vegetables, spices, coffees and teas.

De Grote Pan 21

Dapperstraat 155

🚋 Trams 3, 7, 10 and 14

Open: Mon–Sat

This place is an *eetcafé* with a little off-street terrace that catches the morning sun. Inside you'll find a neighbour-hood bar which sells mainly sandwiches but there are dozens to choose from, as well as the usual range of drinks.

Krijner 22

Dapperstraat 157

🚋 Trams 3, 7, 10 and 14

Open: Mon–Sat

Another European deli with a good range of cheeses and cold meats.

Osmandi 23

Dapperstraat 94

🚋 Trams 3, 7, 10 and 14

Open: Mon–Sat

A Turkish bakery selling rolls, loaves and confec-tioneries. You won't be able to resist the delightful smell of fresh bread as you walk by.

Markets

Dappermarkt 24

Dapperstraat

🚋 Trams 3, 7, 10 and 14

Open: Mon–Sat

The food stalls increase as you get further south in this enjoyable but lesser-known market in the east of the city. There are several cheese stalls, plus fish, fruit and vegetable stalls too, including some with exotic fruits reflecting the mixed Asian-Middle

Eastern-African neighbourhood. You could dine off roast chicken or snack at one of the stalls selling *falafels* or Vietnamese fast food, or make yourself a picnic lunch to take to the nearby Oosterpark from the market or from the many food shops that line the same street, Dapperstraat.

▲ Dappermarkt

Picnic sites

Botanical Gardens 25

🚊 Trams 9, 14 and 20

The Hortus Botanicus has been here since 1682 and, although there is a small admission charge, it makes a great place to combine sightseeing and a picnic, or you could also dine in the small cafeteria here. Children will enjoy seeing the terrapins and the Venus flytraps, while adults will appreciate the 6 000 different plant species.

Oosterpark 26

🚊 Trams 6, 9, 10, 14 and 20

Open: Mon–Sat

The large and delightful Oosterpark is a great place to head if you are visiting the nearby **zoo** or **Children's Museum**. It is just far enough out of the city centre to keep it free of too many tourists, and there is usually plenty of space to settle down with a picnic. Children can enjoy the small play area around a sandpit, and there is also a small lake to enhance the view.

Wertheim Park 27

🚊 Trams 9, 14 and 20

This small park on the opposite side of the road from the **Botanical Gardens** and alongside the Nieuwe Herengracht canal has a fountain and park benches at one end and the moving **Auschwitz Monument** at the other. The inscription reads 'Auschwitz – Never Again'.

▲ Oosterpark

Dutch cheese

Tourism borne upon tradition

The Dutch love cheese, of that there is no doubt. They are also very successful at exporting it, to the extent of some 400,000 tonnes a year, and they also supply Greece with about 80 per cent of its allegedly homemade Greek feta cheese. It can come as a surprise to visitors to discover that their two best-known types of cheese, Edam and Gouda, are in fact real places. They are both easily accessible from Amsterdam, and their cheese markets – even though heavily reliant on the tourist trade – make a day trip to either well worthwhile.

Edam is only about 10km north of the city centre and can be reached by taking a number 110, 112 or 114 bus, all of which leave roughly hourly from outside the Centraal Station (the correct pronunciation is 'Ay-dam', not 'Ee-dam', by the way).

▲ Cheese stall

On Wednesdays in July and August there is a cheese market from 1000 until 1200, where the famous cheese is available in great abundance. You soon discover that the red skin which is famous around the world is for export only, as the version sold in Holland has a yellow skin.

The market takes place, naturally enough, in the **Kaasmarkt** (Cheese Market), which was a real cheese market until 1922 but these days only caters to the visitors. Also in the Kaasmarkt you will find the old 16th-century **Kaaswaag**, or 'cheese-weighing house', with its cheese-making display (*open: daily Apr–Oct 1000–1700*). The town does have other attractions, including canals with their drawbridges and canalside houses, old buildings and museums, so passing a day here before taking the short ride back to Amsterdam is easily done.

So too is visiting **Gouda** (pronounced 'how-der'), which is 30km southwest of the centre and reached by train from the Centraal Station. Gouda is an exceedingly attractive place in its own right, and its cheese market takes place on Thursdays from June to August, from 0930 until 1200, neatly avoiding a clash with the market at Edam. Here too the cheese market was genuine, before dying out and only being kept alive by tourism. Hundreds of local farmers would descend on the market, bringing their Gouda with them to be weighed, tested and graded before hoping to strike a bargain with a wholesaler who would take the cheeses to Amsterdam and beyond. The *markt* where the cheese market is held is the largest market square in Holland, and in addition to this impressive sight, the town also boasts elegant canals and attendant bridges and houses, numerous old buildings and a couple of museums.

The best cheese market of all, though, is probably the one at **Alkmaar**, some 37km northwest of Amsterdam, and reached in an hour by trains which leave Centraal Station about once an hour. This is the least well known of the 'Dutch Cheese Towns' to outsiders but has been synonymous with the cheese trade in Holland for the last 700 years. This market takes place on Friday mornings from April until September, and although like the ones at Edam and Gouda it is firmly aimed at the tourist market, at Alkmaar they put on a bit more of a show with people dressed in traditional costumes, running round with their cheeses, and here too you will see the traditional Dutch method of trading cheeses. The price is agreed not verbally but by a series of hand-claps, finally sealed by one solid hand-clap, after which the cheese will be taken for weighing.

> **The price is agreed not verbally but by a series of hand-claps, finally sealed by one solid hand-clap, after which the cheese will be taken for weighing.**

It would be a shame if you visited Amsterdam and only stuck to the famous names that you knew, when sampling cheeses. Edam and Gouda are really among the least impressive of Dutch cheeses, although even these can show startling variety, depending on whether they are *jong* (young), *belegen* (mature) or *oud* (old). Try a *leidse*, which is a Gouda that has been flavoured with cumin seeds, or *nagelkaas*, which is a cheese flavoured with cloves and sometimes cumin as well.

Holland's neighbours, the Belgians, have complained that they make hundreds of excellent cheeses and no one anywhere in the world can name a single one of them. The Dutch, however, have succeeded in making export successes of two of the most bland cheeses ever produced, in Holland or anywhere else: Edam and Gouda. Once you have tried other Dutch cheeses, you might start to wonder whether they are not simply keeping the best ones for themselves.

Food etiquette and culture

TYPES OF ESTABLISHMENT

In Amsterdam more than anywhere, definitions of eating places are blurred. At least a restaurant is a restaurant, but beyond that there are numerous options. To begin with, a coffeeshop is not simply a coffeeshop but is the name for places where soft drugs can be legally bought and consumed, as well as the usual coffees, beers and so on.

If you don't want the soft drug menu option, then go to a café. Most serve cold snacks and some serve hot meals, although there is also an *eetcafé* where a much wider range of meals will be available. Tearooms may concentrate on tea but the name is also frequently used by cafés that simply don't want to call themselves coffeeshops.

Then there are brown bars and brown cafés, named after the colour of the walls after years, and sometimes centuries, of cigarette smoke have had their effect. Both will usually serve food of some kind, some more successfully than others; a café will simply have more emphasis on soft drinks, a bar on alcoholic drinks.

Proeflokalen is the Dutch word for a tasting house, although there aren't too many of them left. They were originally the tasting houses for distillers, primarily producing the Dutch *jenever* (see page 56), but the word was borrowed to describe any such place, whether linked to a distillery or not. The few remaining ones sell spirits almost exclusively, and generally close early in the evening.

WHEN TO EAT

Lunch is taken from about noon onwards, and many small places may well be full as early as 1230. The Dutch also tend to eat early in the evening, anything from about 1800 onwards, and many restaurants will be winding down by 2200, if they are not closed altogether. It's not unusual for a bar or restaurant to open at 1700, although there will still be plenty of customers turning up for tables at 2000 and later.

BREAKFAST

Breakfast is normally included in the cost of a hotel room, and in larger hotels this will take the form of a buffet of cold meats, cheeses, a choice of breads, probably fruit and yoghurt too,

and either tea or coffee. In smaller hotels where the breakfast is served at table, you will usually receive a decent basic meal, though seldom extravagant, of ham and cheese, toast, a boiled egg, various breads and preserves, plus tea, coffee or hot chocolate. Note that orange juice isn't as common on the Dutch breakfast table as it is elsewhere in the world. You may have to ask for it.

HOT DRINKS

Most restaurants, cafés and bars will have a good range of teas available, thanks to Holland's historical connections with the Far East, and this will usually include a wide choice of herbal teas, given the Dutch interest in a healthy lifestyle. Dutch tea is often served with lemon rather than milk, so do ask for tea with milk if that's what you want.

If you simply ask for a coffee you will probably be served a black one, in a very small cup. Ask for coffee with milk and you will usually be given an extremely milky drink indeed, so if you want white coffee ask for a small amount of milk or ask for milk on the side, to pour in yourself.

Hot chocolate is almost as popular as tea and coffee, and is drunk from breakfast through to suppertime – you will usually have to say whether you want it hot or cold.

LIQUEURS

If you order a liqueur in a brown café and find that it is put in front of you seemingly too full to lift the glass without spilling some of

the contents, remember that it is the Dutch custom to fill the glass to the very top so that you have to lean over and slurp some out of it before you can pick it up. If you still have trouble picking it up maybe it's a sign that you've done too much slurping!

TIPPING

Tipping is not part of Dutch culture, so don't feel obliged to add ten per cent. Rounding up to the nearest five or ten guilders is normal for larger amounts, or leaving the small change after a drink or two. By law all establishments should include a 15 per cent service charge built into the bill. By all means leave a little extra tip if you have had exceptionally good service, and while it is appreciated, it is not expected.

Menu decoder

MEALS AND GENERAL TERMS
ontbijt – breakfast
lunch – lunch
diner – dinner
bediening – service
bijgerecht – side dish
boterham – sandwich
gerecht – dish or course
hapje – snack
koffietafel – a cold buffet lunch
nagerecht – dessert
spijskaart – menu
voorgerecht – starter

COOKING METHODS
blauw – rare
doorbakken – well done
gebakken – fried
gebraden – roast
gekookt – boiled
gemarineerd – marinated
gerookt/gerookte – smoked
geroosterd – grilled
gestoofd – stewed
pocheren – poached

DRESSINGS
azijn – vinegar
madera saus – brown sauce made with Madeira wine
mosterd – mustard
olijfolie – olive oil
saus – sauce
slaolie – salad oil
slasaus – salad cream

BREADS
belegde broodje – a filled roll
brood – bread
broodje – roll
geroosterd brood – toast
kadetje – a soft roll
oliebol – doughnut
roggebrood – rye bread
stokbrood – baguette
tarwebrood – wheat bread
tosti/toastie – toasted sandwich
volkorenbrood – wholemeal bread
wafel – waffle or wafer
wittebrood – white bread

STARTERS AND SUNDRY DISHES
bitterballen – croquettes, deep-fried with a cheese filling
boerenomelet – omelette with ham and potatoes

boterham met kaas – cheese
  sandwich
chips – crisps
chocoladepasta – chocolate
  spread
eieren – eggs
honing – honey
huzarensalade – potato salad
  served with gherkins,
  beetroot, onions, sardines
  or other embellishments
kroketten – croquettes, deep-
  fried with a meat filling
koekjes – biscuits
olijven (groene/zwarte) –
  olives (green/black)
pannekoek – pancake; *met
  jam* (with jam), *met
  stroop* (with syrup), *met
  suiker* (with sugar)
poffertjes – small thick
  pancakes which are
  sweet, and covered in
  icing sugar
rijst – rice
roerei – scrambled eggs
room – cream
roomboter – dairy butter
slaatje – salad
soep van de dag – soup of the
  day
spiegelei – fried egg
uitsmijter – open sandwich with
  meat or cheese, and with a
  fried egg on top

FISH AND SEAFOOD
ansjovissen – anchovies
forel – trout
garnalencocktail – prawn cocktail
haring – herring
kabeljauw – cod
kreeft – lobster
lekkerbekjes – whiting deep-fried
  in batter
mosselen – mussels
oesters – oysters
sardientjes – sardines

schartong – lemon sole
schelvis – haddock
schol – plaice
tonijn – tuna
vis – fish
zalm – salmon

MEAT DISHES
biefstuk – beefsteak; *der haas*
  (fillet), *der lende* (rump/sirloin)
bloedworst – black pudding
frikadellen – spicy meat-balls
  made with minced meat
gehakt – mince
hertevlees – venison
hutspot – hotpot, or stew, usually
  of beef and vegetables
jachschotel – shepherd's pie
kalfslever – calf's liver
kalfsvlees – veal
kalkoen – turkey
karbonade – chop

kip – chicken
knackworst – frankfurter
nieren – kidneys
ontbijtspek – bacon
ossestaart – oxtail
paarderookvlees – smoked
    horsemeat
rundervlees – beef
schwarmas/shoarmas – kebabs
slavinken – minced pork wrapped
    in bacon
varkensvlees – pork
zoutjes – savoury meatballs
zuurkool – sauerkraut

HERBS, NUTS, PULSES AND VEGETABLES
aardappelen – potatoes
artisjok – artichoke
asperges – asparagus
augerken – gherkin
bieten – beetroot
bloemkool – cauliflower
champignon – mushroom
doperwten – garden peas
groenten – vegetables
hete bliksem – a mash of
    potatoes and apples

knoflook – garlic
kool – cabbage
kruiden – herbs
linzen – lentils
mierik – horseradish
patates frites – chips/French fries
    or *pommes frites*
peper – pepper
prie – leek
specerijen – spices
sperziebonen – French beans
spinazie – spinach
uien – onions
vlaamse frites – chips (literally
    'Flemish fries')

FRUIT
aardbiein – strawberries
ananas – pineapple
appel – apple
banaan – banana
citroen – lemon
druiven (witte/blauwe) – grapes
    (white/black)
frambozen – raspberries
kersen – cherries
perziken – peaches
pompelmoes – grapefruit

pruimen – plums
sinaasappel – orange

DESSERTS AND CHEESE
boerenjongens – brandy
  with raisins
boerenmeisjes – apricots in
  brandy
boerenkaas – farmhouse
  cheese
chocoladevla – chocolate
  custard
dame blanche – ice cream
  with chocolate sauce
edammer – Edam cheese
gebakje – small cake
goudse kaas – Gouda cheese
kaas – cheese
kwarktaart – cheesecake
rijstebrij – rice pudding
roomijs – ice cream
schuimpje – meringue
slagroom – whipped cream
taart – cake
vanillevla – custard sauce
vruchtensla – fruit salad

DRINKS
advocaat – eggnog
appelsap – apple juice
bessenjenever – blackcurrant
  liqueur
bier – beer
bier van het vat – draught beer
brandewijn – brandy
chocomel – a commercial
  chocolate drink, tinned or
  bottled
droog – dry or *sec*
gedistilleerde dranken – spirits or
  spirituosa
jenever – Dutch gin, flavoured
  with juniper berries
kafe verkeerd – weak coffee with
  milk
koffie – coffee
korenwijn – top quality matured
  gin

kwast – lemon squash
landwijn – table wine
limonade – lemonade
melk – milk, *magere* (skimmed),
  halfvolle (semi-skimmed)
pils – type of lager beer
port – port
sinaasappelsap – orange juice
spa water – mineral water
vermout – vermouth
vruchtensap – fruit juice
wijn – wine *witte/rode* (white/red)
zoet – sweet

For Indonesian food definitions
see page 77.

Recipes

Although Dutch cooking is not in the same European league as French, Italian or Spanish, say, it does have many of its own distinctive recipes. The best of these are probably for fish and meat dishes, especially game, but the two included here are both uniquely Dutch. Pancakes are available throughout Amsterdam, and it's the sign of a truly national dish that it will appear in the most humble of eating places and yet also on the menus of gourmet restaurants, where they try to show just how well they can prepare it. Advocaat is also uniquely Dutch, and although it can easily be bought, there is nothing to equal being able to tailor-make and then refine your own particular version. Here is a basic recipe to set you on your way.

Pannekoeken (Dutch Pancakes)

Serves 1

INGREDIENTS

500g wheat flour	
1 litre milk	
4 medium eggs	
1 tsp salt	
1 tblsp oil	
1 tsp sugar	
butter	

Prepare the mixture by hand or in a food processor. If by hand, first put the flour in a bowl, make a hole in the middle, pour in some milk and start stirring. Gradually pour in all of the milk to make a smooth mixture. Break the eggs and mix them in one at a time, and then add the salt, the sugar and the oil and keep mixing until the batter is smooth with no lumps.

Heat the butter in a frying pan until it starts

to brown and then pour in about 2 to 3 tablespoons of batter. If you don't like to use butter you can use oil, but it must be very hot before pouring in the batter. When the upper surface of the pancake becomes dry, flip the pancake and cook the other side for the same amount of time. You can turn it using a spatula or try flipping it in the air if you're feeling bold.

While the second half is cooking, add your filling. The Dutch use almost anything. Bacon pancakes are popular, though for these you must fry the bacon first and then pour the batter over it. You might also try this with mushrooms, smoked sausage or vegetables.

If you want a sweet pancake then these are usually served with Dutch syrup, or use American or maple syrup. Fruit fillings are also popular, especially cherries. For apple pancakes fry chunks of apple in the pan first, before adding the batter mix. Adding a touch of alcohol towards the end is popular: try calvados or brandy.

Advocaat (Dutch eggnog)

Serves 10–12

INGREDIENTS

10 eggs
4 double cognacs
275g sugar
½ level teaspoon of salt
½ level teaspoon of vanilla essence or extract

Separate the eggs and beat the salt and sugar into the yolks until the mixture is thick and creamy. Then beat in the cognac a little at a time and when it is all beaten in, put the mixture into a large saucepan. Heat it gently and keep beating until the mixture is warm and thick, but do not let it get too hot. Remove from the heat and then stir in the vanilla extract or essence. Pour it into a jug to cool and then serve it in dessert glasses, to be eaten with a spoon. It can also be served with a topping of whipped cream.

Published by Thomas Cook Publishing
Thomas Cook Holdings Ltd
PO Box 227
Thorpe Wood
Peterborough PE3 6PU
United Kingdom

Telephone: 01733 503571
Email: books@thomascook.com

Text © 2001 Thomas Cook Publishing
Maps © 2001 Thomas Cook Publishing

ISBN 1 841570 51 6

Distributed in the United States of
America by the Globe Pequot Press,
PO Box 480, Guilford, Connecticut
06437, USA

Publisher: Donald Greig
Commissioning Editor: Deborah Parker
Map Editor: Bernard Horton

Project management: Dial House
    Publishing
Series Editor: Christopher Catling
Copy Editor: Lucy Thomson
Proofreader: Jan Wiltshire

Series and cover design: WhiteLight
Cover artwork: WhiteLight and
    Kaarin Wall
Text layout: SJM Design Consultancy,
    Dial House Publishing
Maps prepared by Polly Senior
    Cartography

Repro and image setting: PDQ Digital
    Media Solutions Ltd
Printed and bound in Italy by
    Eurografica SpA

Written and researched by **Mike Gerrard**

We would like to thank the author for the
photographs used in this book, to whom
the copyright belongs, with the exception
of the following:
Paul Murphy (pages 56 and 94)
Eddy Posthuma de Boer (page 47)
Neil Setchfield (pages 9, 10, 13, 14, 15, 20,
23, 24, 25, 26, 27, 29, 33, 40, 41, 42, 43,
44, 45, 50, 51, 53, 54, 55, 57, 59, 70, 71,
73, 74, 75, 77 and 95).